GW01339921

BADIOU BY BADIOU

Cultural Memory
 in
 the
Present

Hent de Vries, Editor

BADIOU BY BADIOU

Alain Badiou

Translated by Bruno Bosteels

Stanford University Press
Stanford, California

STANFORD UNIVERSITY PRESS
Stanford, California

English translation ©2022 by the Board of Trustees of the Leland Stanford Junior University. All rights reserved.

Badiou by Badiou was originally published in French in 2021 under the title *Alain Badiou par Alain Badiou* ©2021, Presses Universitaires de France / Humensis.

No part of this book may be reproduced or transmitted in any form or by any means, electronic or mechanical, including photocopying and recording, or in any information storage or retrieval system without the prior written permission of Stanford University Press.

Printed in the United States of America on acid-free, archival-quality paper

Library of Congress Cataloging-in-Publication Data

Names: Badiou, Alain, author. | Bosteels, Bruno, translator.
Title: Badiou by Badiou / Alain Badiou ; translated by Bruno Bosteels.
Other titles: Alain Badiou par Alain Badiou. English | Cultural memory in the present.
Description: Stanford, California : Stanford University Press, 2022. | Series: Cultural memory in the present | "Originally published in French in 2021 under the title Alain Badiou par Alain Badiou."
Identifiers: LCCN 2021049464 (print) | LCCN 2021049465 (ebook) | ISBN 9781503630338 (cloth) | ISBN 9781503631762 (paperback) | ISBN 9781503631779 (ebook)
Subjects: LCSH: Badiou, Alain. | Badiou, Alain—Interviews. | Mathematics—Philosophy. | LCGFT: Lectures. | Interviews.
Classification: LCC B2430.B272 E5 2022 (print) | LCC B2430.B272 (ebook) | DDC 194—dc23/eng/20211104
LC record available at https://lccn.loc.gov/2021049464
LC ebook record available at https://lccn.loc.gov/2021049465

Cover design: Rob Ehle

Text design: Kevin Barrett Kane

Typeset at Stanford University Press in 11/14.4 Adobe Garamond Pro

Contents

Preface ix

PART ONE
Event, Truths, Subject   1

I   What Is Philosophy?   1

II The Conditions of Philosophy:
    Sciences, Arts, Love, and Politics   4

III The "Truth Procedure":
    *Some Key Concepts: Being and Event,
    Subject and Fidelity*   10

IV The History of Philosophy:
    From Plato to Wittgenstein   18

V   "Changing the World" /
    "Corrupting the Youth"   25

VI	Equality, Universality, Emancipation: *The Communist Idea*	30

PART TWO
Philosophy Between Mathematics and Poetry 36

PART THREE
Ontology and Mathematics 48

I	Philosophy and Its Conditions	48
II	"In the Situation"	50
III	Ontologies	53
IV	Being and Event	58
V	Logics of Worlds	67
VI	The Immanence of Truths	77

Preface

The present book is the result of a considerable effort on the part of a few Flemish friends, who touched me deeply by wanting my work to become a clear and constant reference for contemporary youth. By "my work," they obviously meant first and foremost the metaphysical trilogy comprised of *Being and Event* (1988), *Logics of Worlds* (2006), and *The Immanence of Truths* (2018). But these are dense and systematic works, and if one seeks to address young people or, generally speaking, as large an audience as possible, it is no doubt necessary to prepare the reading of those works with some preliminary explanations. With this aim in mind and to provide a point of entry into the trilogy, the friends in question, who are also exemplary teachers, opted for more didactic and accessible means of communication: the lecture and the interview. In the vast corpus of such materials, they have, without making the least concession to demagoguery, privileged those texts that in their eyes combine conceptual clarity with the power of synthetic vision. Thus, they were able to do justice to the central questions of my philosophical project—being and universality, worlds and singularity, the event, the subject and truths, the infinite and the absolute—while at the same time attending to the continuity between these notions and the essential creative practices of which the human animal has proven capable: the sciences, and especially mathematics; the arts, especially poetry; politics, especially communism; and, finally, love as the unique concern for the being of the other.

The combination of the texts chosen by the authors of this montage represents an orderly kind of journey across my entire philosophical endeavor. I do not think there exists anything comparable today, and I can say that by reading the ensemble, by re-reading it, I learned a great deal about myself. This goes to show that a genuine concern for the other, for the transmission of thought to the other, is indispensable for entering into any body of thought. This is also why I have a vivid memory of the encounter that took place in Brussels, organized by those same friends responsible for the present book, with a group of high school students who made me understand by their gaze, their attention, and their questions that they were in the process of giving me, as author, a lively existence both in their consciousness and in their own projects.

Many thanks are therefore due to my friends for offering me and everyone else this unexpected and persuasive composite picture of the project to which I have devoted an essential part of my thought, my lectures, and my writings.

Alain Badiou

BADIOU BY BADIOU

PART ONE

Event, Truths, Subject

I. WHAT IS PHILOSOPHY?

We would like to begin this interview with a few general questions: what is philosophy for you, or according to you? And why philosophy?

I will first give a personal and then a general answer. Because philosophy for me has been an encounter, the encounter of a master-teacher. I think that philosophy remains tied to the figure of the philosopher. Besides, Lacan used to say that philosophy is situated on the side of the discourse of the master. He did not mean this by way of praise, but that is how I assume it. I am not bothered by this. When I was still very young—at the age of 16 or 17—I was completely blown away and transformed by the experience of the reading of Sartre. So, subjectively speaking, philosophy for me has been first of all the encounter with a type of discourse of which I wanted to follow the indications and develop the consequences.

We are indeed dealing with a discourse that has the peculiar feature of bearing directly on the existence of the subject as such. It is not something that can be taught to the subject. It is something aimed at transforming the subject's worldview, distinguishing between good and bad actions, and so on. From this point of view, since there exists a figure of the philosopher, philosophy is not a general discourse. It is a discourse that is both subjective, or subjectivized, and, at the same time, tries to transform those to whom it is addressed. This truly fascinated me. At the time I wanted to be either an inspector of forests and waterways or a comedian, and, finally, because of Sartre, I switched over to the side of philosophy.

On this basis, how would I define philosophy as I received and understood it beyond Sartre, who has been my first teacher? For I did not abandon him afterwards; I simply went beyond or did something else. But how, then, do I represent philosophy in itself? The legitimacy of its existence? Why does it exist? And why am I a philosopher?

Philosophy actually tries to extract from among all human activities those that have or may have a universal value. I think that is right—even when we are dealing with critical or skeptical philosophies, they are skeptical about this very question. They may well conclude that we will not arrive at an answer to the question, but it is nonetheless their question as well. For example, the skeptics say that we cannot know the truth, but this is because in reality they are interested in the truth. So, their question concerns the truth, and afterwards their personal drama consists in not being able to know the truth, but this remains a philosophical option. Overall, this is what philosophy is.

It is a kind of central hub, busy with everything in human activity, in human thought, and in human creation that may have a transmissible, universal value—including those philosophies that conclude that this search is impossible or difficult. They, too, are part of philosophy because they bear witness to the same question. That is how I see philosophy.

By the same token, it seems to me that a characteristic feature of philosophy concerns the mode of its transmission. The transmission of philosophy constitutes a crucial question, which is part of philosophy and has been much discussed by the philosophers. In today's world, I think there are two paths with regard to this topic. There is a first path, which considers that finally philosophy can be an academic discipline. And so, its transmission will be the same as that of geography, or of history. This itself has a long history: Aristotle, who is a very great philosopher, already thought in this way. He thought there was a master-teacher, and the latter created a school. This also shows up in his style, because Aristotle always starts out from a clear definition and then he draws out the consequences of what others have said before him.

And then, there exists a second path, which considers that philosophy involves a subjectivization, that it presupposes points of anchoring that far exceed the possibilities of academic disciplines. What does one do, for example, with the youth when one busies oneself with philosophy? It cannot be a strictly academic affair: something else must be invented, a situation must be created. The transmission of philosophy is always the creation of situations in which the addressee has the feeling of encountering something. The other disciplines can be taught. Philosophy cannot be taught, properly speaking; it must be encountered and that is what makes up its singularity.

In life you may have the good fortune of encountering philosophy, and you may have the misfortune of not encountering it. I see a lot of students at the university who belong to the department of philosophy, and after talking with them for five minutes, I see that they have yet to encounter philosophy. But there are some who have encountered it.

So, if you ask me for a definition, I will say that philosophy exists when one encounters the existence of a possibility, the possibility of traversing and examining that of which humanity is capable, and then seeing if this has value or not.

II. THE CONDITIONS OF PHILOSOPHY: SCIENCES, ARTS, LOVE, AND POLITICS

The sciences, the arts, love, and politics . . . In your system there are four conditions of philosophy—how should we think of this conditioning of philosophy? How are the four conditions of philosophy linked to one another? Could you explain this by giving an example for each condition?

This question can be linked to the previous one: if philosophy is the investigation of that of which humanity is capable, including in terms of the worst—the fact that humankind is capable of awful things also interests the philosopher—if that is what philosophy is, then we must turn toward humanity's actual creative practices. In other words, it does not belong to philosophy itself to invent what humanity is capable of. Philosophy simply searches for that which humanity is capable of and asks what distinguishes it in this regard. What is better or the best? The source of philosophy thus lies outside of philosophy. Now, I have chosen to use the old term "truth" to designate that of which humanity is capable, which possibly has a universal value. Let us say that it concerns everything that humanity is capable of and that, in a certain way, can be and even must be transmitted in general, to the entire world.

It seems to me that one could classify these creations of humankind according to their singularity into four groups. I have called them the four "conditions" of philosophy, insofar as philosophy is conditioned by the fact of there being something that humanity is capable of. Otherwise, it has no reason to be. I therefore have proposed a first broad classification in which I place, on the one hand, that which directly takes the form of a subjective commitment. In this category I include politics, as a form of collective commitment, and love, as a form of individual commitment. On the other hand, there is the objective production of something: it can be a book, a text, a theorem, but it is transmitted in the form of something that truly exists. The first figure describes love and politics; and here, in the second figure, this would be the case of the arts and the sciences. From this follows my thesis that there are four types of conditions of philosophy, which are the sciences, artistic practices, politics, and love—leaving room for later to come back to each of them separately and to specify, study, and interrogate the possible links or the texture of the system among philosophy's four conditions.

Now if we are to give an example for each condition, ultimately this is not too complicated because the examples are well known and ordinary. I am not looking for exceptional examples. In the figure of science, it is mathematics that obviously constitutes my privileged object. It is a condition of philosophy because, in my view, and this issue is very important, mathematics announces that the truth of which it is the bearer is immediately universal; it does not depend on a single creator. This does not mean that there are no great mathematicians, but, as soon as their work exists, it is immediately common to all. Why? Because if one accepts the proposed axioms, one is forced to admit the consequences as well: there is no escape. In other words, mathematics is not debatable in the proper sense of the word: it establishes a field of knowledge that is beyond dispute. Of course, this is fascinating for philosophy, because what is beyond dispute seems to be totally exceptional and remarkable. Moreover, I want to stress that philosophy is born in Greece at the same time as mathematics and that it has not ceased being intertwined with mathematics ever since. Obviously, this is only one example: there are also major discoveries in physics, in biology . . . My philosophy has privileged mathematics, just as many other philosophies have. But you find great philosophers who have privileged biology, for example. Take Bergson: he is someone for whom Darwin, with the movement of life, constitutes an essential reference point.

If now we take the arts, we immediately see that poetry in its most general sense plays a major role in the whole history of philosophy, particularly if one includes theater among the poetic disciplines. Plato's entire oeuvre is involved in an extremely complicated debate around this question. Besides, in my eyes it would be very interesting to obtain a complete and precise analysis of Plato's relationship to the theater, which is something that has not yet been done. This is a debate in which philosophy confronts a condition and meets it with suspicion because it admires it too much, and suspects that its seductive power is perhaps too singular, or insufficiently universal. But everyone can see the convoluted and complex debate that Plato has regarding the theater. It is a debate with a condition recognized as such: he would not spend all this time discussing the theater if the latter were not precisely one of the conditions of philosophy, and, moreover, a condition whose temptation he himself has felt, since it is always said, without any proof, that Plato in his youth wrote some tragedies and burned them after he met Socrates. In my opinion, this is a made-up story, but it is a story with a didactic value. As for myself, I end up privileging both poetry and theater, but this is a choice that demands a particular kind of philosophical labor. There are excellent efforts out there to place philosophy under the condition of painting, for example. Even in the case of Sartre, who wrote a great book on Tintoretto. And obviously this is also the case of Merleau-Ponty. So when it comes to the arts, it can also be painting, or architecture, or dance.

Regarding the relation between these first two conditions, in the case of mathematics it is the idea of its immediate universality that fascinates me; and in the case of the arts, in general, it is the fact that all of a sudden, the sensible acquires a certain value. It is a bit the opposite of mathematics, but it is the possible universality of the sensible. Otherwise, the sensible is there: it is this table, the cup of coffee, you three. Apparently, it is nothing at all, for there is no creation of universal value in the fact that the four of us are sitting and talking around this table. Thus, one can certainly understand why the sensible has always been suspect in the eyes of the philosophers for falling outside the system of the four conditions. Nevertheless, we must recognize a Beethoven symphony or a great painting as something sensible. There is no escaping this fact. The sensible, itself reworked in unique conditions, may take the figure of something with a universal value; it can be one of the creations of humanity that is utterly striking and gripping, oriented toward universality. Therefore, the arts are proof of the fact that the sensible itself can be elaborated and lifted to the height of a universal value, even as it is the immediate representation of that which is not universal but on the contrary totally particular.

So much for the sciences and the arts. With regard to love, on the other hand, I am often asked the question: what does love have to do with all this? Love is my private life. And here we find a link between two conditions, because art, for its part, realized very early on that love had a universal bearing and pleaded in favor of love. If we were to suppress love, the number of artworks that would disappear would be quite considerable. We must state the obvious: art itself has felt that there was something on the side of love that despite everything constituted an exception to the general affectivity of humankind and that love was of interest to all. This has been true throughout the centuries, with all those love stories. And so, one may ask oneself: what happens when everybody is fascinated by Romeo and Juliet, or by Tristan and Isolde? One certainly senses that this is because there is something in the nature of love that exceeds precisely the singularity of affect, all the while being *within* the singularity of affect. And from this point of view, I would say that love is to affect—to the sensible relationship with the other—what art is to the sensible in general. That is, art works with the sensible in general and transforms it into a creation, and I think that love works with the affects—humanity's passionate capacity—and produces a universal meaning as their result.

Every love relationship is a veritable invention, a creation that places humankind beyond the pure and simple reproductive function of sexuality. It must be said that sexuality is certainly at stake: in the end, love is the sublimation of sexuality, not in the sense of its negation—even though this is a tendency in philosophy—but on the contrary in the sense of its exaltation, its affirmation. And, in this sense, I think that it is a condition of philosophy. And I am particularly an admirer of Plato, for many reasons, but in this instance I admire him for having said and written that whoever has not been in love cannot be a philosopher. The phrase is there, without a doubt. It has not provoked a great amount of explanation, even though there has been a lot of talk of Platonic love, in versions that are as false as they are anti-sexual, whereas this is not at all what Plato tells us.

And, finally, there is politics. Now in politics it is once again the same question: what is it in, let us say, the Neolithic organization of societies—in a collective organization that puts in place figures of constraint, figures of organization of the collective, but also figures of violence, figures of rivalry—what is it in all this that finally may appear at a given moment as a creation with a truly universal signification? I would say that, from the start, it is when politics proves capable of overcoming the immediate differences between human beings and addressing humanity in its entirety. And on this point, of course, what remains of history divides itself into two: there is the history of historians who tell us what happened, and they, evidently, tell us about the contingencies of the struggle for power, because that is what is the most visible. And then there is the way in which all this may function as a condition for philosophy, which on the contrary concerns all the episodes that oppose power with another value. Philosophy has broadly named this value "justice," that is, all that has been the human effort to organize the collective according to a norm of justice and not according to a norm of efficacy, productivity, or hierarchy. Everything that has gone in this direction explains why a philosophical hero may be Spartacus, it may be Robespierre, it may be the popular masses in such and such a circumstance. This has been of vital interest to philosophy from the beginning, because of all the things that philosophy cannot tolerate, it is that the social order, which is one of humanity's creations, should be subordinated to the principle of personal interest. I for one would say that politics is the moment when one attempts to act in such a way as to reflect on the conditions in which the principle of personal interest would not be the driving force of political organization.

III. THE "TRUTH PROCEDURE": SOME KEY CONCEPTS: BEING AND EVENT, SUBJECT AND FIDELITY

After discussing philosophy and its four conditions, we now would like to focus on a few key concepts in your thinking. We looked for an accessible point of entry that would be understandable to the public at large and to our audience of 17- or 18-year-old students, and we concluded that what you call "truth procedure" offers a good point of departure. This is even more helpful as this concept allows us to talk about being, about the event and its consequences—namely, truth, the subject, and fidelity.

I think this is a good point of departure, because in the end there is a certain simplicity to all this.

"Truth" is the general name that philosophy gives to the ensemble of what we just discussed, namely, the ensemble of the productions in time and space of something that may, for solid reasons, assume to have a universal value. Certainly, this is a rather peculiar meaning of the word "truth," because usually truth is when I say something true instead of telling a joke. Such is the ordinary meaning of the word "truth." However, in our case we are beyond all that because truth can also be a painting by Picasso, the Bolshevik Revolution, *Romeo and Juliet*, or the Pythagorean theorem—all of which are examples of truths. Thus, I take "truth" in a broader sense, which prevents us from reducing "truth" to how it is used in language, which is the narrow and academic version of the word "truth," reduced to the question of whether a proposition is true or false. I take "truth" from the beginning in a much larger sense, which includes the truths of mathematics but also many other things.

The point in need of clarification is how it is possible for there to be an exceptional creation. For there are truths, even lots of them, and we know that in a certain sense they are all exceptional things. By "exceptional" I understand "what is not a normal, or natural, product of the existing state of affairs." If we go back to our examples, we can clearly see this: a great love is not the same thing as a little affair with someone. A revolution is not the same thing as a state power, installed in its tranquility and corruption. A great painting is not the same thing as some daubing. And a mathematical theorem is not the same thing as a simple calculation to know the price of a machine. Thus, there is clearly something exceptional in truths in general, whatever they may be. But what does this mean? That is where the properly philosophical interrogation begins.

What does it mean for something to be exceptional? It means that it was not foreseeable within the general laws of what exists. We can also say that something is ordinary and not exceptional when it can be explained simply by the established laws of the existing world. There exist countless things for which we can explain perfectly well why they exist, and those are the ordinary phenomena of the world. They are foreign to the question of true and false. They exist, that's all, and their existence has nothing to do with the exceptionality of the true, any more than with the false. They are neither false nor true: they are there, that's all.

Thus, at the origin of a truth there must be something that is not reducible to the strict determinations and laws of the world in which it has been produced. On the other hand, this production always occurs in a determinate world; it does not come from heaven, it is not a god, it is not an *other* world: it takes place *within* the world. A sequence of true politics, a great love, take place in a determinate world and thus must be "immanent" to this world, to use a slightly rough-sounding term, which means "internal to a given world." And it also must be an exception to the laws of the world, since the laws of the world do not permit us to predict it. Thus, if we examine all this in general, the philosophical problem is the problem of what I have called an "immanent exception." And that is what a truth is: a truth is an immanent exception. And it is universal, because it is an exception: if it were strictly immanent, we would only be able to understand it from within the world in question. If it can be understood in another world, this is precisely because it is an exception to the world in which it takes place, even though it is made with materials and things from this very world. Consequently, at the origin of a genuine creation we find something that, while being *in* the world, is not exactly *of* the world, and this is what I have called an "event." An event is something that takes place in the world but is not calculable on the basis of the elements of this world itself. It happens. What distinguishes the event from being—as in *Being and Event*, the title of my first major book of philosophy—is that we cannot say that it happens in accordance with the laws of being, but we also cannot say that it happens elsewhere. And so, what distinguishes being and event is that the event exists in the world as taking placing or happening in a world, whereas being supports the reality of the world such as it is. That is the point of origin: there necessarily is an event at the origin of every exceptional novelty, immanent to a determinate world.

But then you will immediately ask me for an example of an event in relation to the different truth procedures! Let us take an event in the realm of painting. It occurs when someone proposes something that treats as a *form* what until then was considered *formless*. The law of the world was that there was a clear distinction between what constitutes a form and what is formless. And then it can happen, and it actually happens, that somebody produces something in which the formless is treated as a form and takes on a form. You can see this for example in the first cubist paintings by Picasso and Braque in the 1910s, but you already see this in the first paintings that detail perspective in Italy in the fifteenth century. Those are some artistic events.

Starting from there, an event will have all kinds of consequences, which are consequences within the world. I call the ensemble of these consequences a "truth procedure." What this makes clear is that the creation of truths can happen entirely within the world—the work and the consequences involved take place inside the world—but at the same time, because of the evental origin of the phenomenon in question, stand apart as an exception, because the work that is implied introduces a tiny, quasi-ontological difference into whatever was recognized as existing in the world. A truth procedure, in the different realms of the four conditions, may be political events, amorous events, artistic events, or scientific events; and, in fact, it is the name I give to those procedures that based on an original event unfold and develop its consequences in the world, thus creating a few immanent exceptions to this world.

It is possible to give all kinds of examples of this. In the realm of love the event can be grasped as pure encounter, that is, the absolute origin of love is when you meet someone. You meet someone and that, in a certain sense, is incalculable, because meetings with different people happen all the time. So then, why should there be one encounter that specifically is capable of creating something that finally has a universal value? This is not something that can be calculated. This is why the crucial moment is when the encounter becomes transformed into an encounter that is declared as such: the love declaration, which is an old story that is also very difficult, a terrible test. Why? Because in actual fact the subject knows that they are entering the exception and that they will have to keep up with it in the amorous procedure. For love is a procedure, which consists of the consequences of the encounter. But the consequences of the encounter, to be at the height of its exceptional character, must be treated as a genuine creation, often on a daily basis.

The situation is similar for all truth procedures. If in the realm of politics you have a massive popular uprising, which completely breaks with the laws of the world, the truth will not be this uprising in and of itself, but the system of political consequences that can be inferred from it, the organization of all this, the appearance of a new path for the general organization of society.

To summarize, a truth procedure requires that something happens, rather than simply being—we are thus in the realm of the arrival or happening in a world, rather than in the order of the calculable being of this world—with the creation and appearing of a "subject," which is going to seize upon this exception and draw from it the consequences that are internal to the world. That is why we are obliged to bring out an agent or actor of all this, a productive power, namely, a subject. The event as such appears and disappears: if you encounter someone, the two of you meet, and then you go your separate ways, and it is as if nothing had happened. In these conditions, which are different each time, a subject must appear who declares what has happened. Love is a good example of this, because you can see very well that the subjective constitution of love takes place from the moment one declares the encounter, when one says "There, I met him or her." And this can be said in different ways, as in "I love you." The language depends on the situation, as do the specific words used.

Here one understands very well that the event as such and its subjective grasp involve a process and that afterwards it will be necessary to draw the endless consequences of this primordial declaration. The same thing happens when there is a break, for example, with Schönberg, who produces a turnabout from the tonal system into a constructive atonality. It is the same thing, because here too it will be necessary to produce new works and create a school to proclaim itself worthy of this orientation. The result will be an atonal kind of music, then a serial one, as the consequences of this mutation, which is to say a creation of truths.

Up to this point, I have spoken simply about the chain of consequences, but obviously what designates the subjective category of the truth procedure for me is the notion of "fidelity." Fidelity is what supports the imperative "Continue!" In the case of love you once again have a very good example, because there can be an initial experience of ecstasy, but the amorous subjectivity is one that proposes to continue, and this is why I have chosen the word "fidelity" to characterize the subject who is a subject of truth properly speaking. A subject of a truth is a subject who is faithful to the inaugural event in the sense of organizing its consequences in the world and according to the laws of the world. And the organization of the consequences according to the laws of the world amounts to a creation of truth, which will create the criteria that we described as the criteria of truth, which as we saw is at the same time immanent and exceptional. But all this can take place only if it is supported by a new subjectivity, which will elaborate precisely the consequences of the event. Thus, a subject is a faithful subject in the sense that it is a subject who works for a truth, and, therefore, this truth in the end can be amorous, scientific, artistic, or political.

In the case of love, "subject" can be quickly understood because it is the subject in the quasi-ordinary sense of the term, meaning the individual subject, who simply is going to become a "two" instead of being "one"—that is to say, a subject who is going to change from "one" into "two" and who will experience and construct the world on the basis of difference, and not on the basis of the self. I often invoke the example of love because it is something everybody knows—more or less, because today there is some skepticism around this issue. But everybody in any case has heard about love. We also see very well that often, in the case of politics, the subject in fact is an organization, which seizes upon a popular event to reinvent its own existence and unfold it in the direction of an egalitarian society delivered from the monstrous hierarchies and inequalities that characterize the world as we know it today.

"Fidelity" is thus the name that in a way designates the consistency and permanence of the subject. And when this fails, becomes interrupted, or comes to an end, when the truth is left in a certain state—for obviously there is a state of the truth, which is tied to the obstinacy of the faithful—even this can still be a creation of truth, albeit interrupted or partial. This is something that we will have to pick up again later in what I call the "resurrection" of truths. The extent of the fidelity is thus variable: you have lovers who love each other until death, which is fidelity at the maximum of its capacity. And then you have political experiences that abort very soon, but that remain a reference point for truth in the future. The typical example is the Paris Commune: it is a segment of just two months in 1871. Nevertheless, its inscription and the projects that were part of the Paris Commune clearly constitute a political paradigm.

Evidently, the faithful subject is the one who, with regard to the event, responds in a way that is immediately positive in the strict sense. This does not mean that everything is great but rather "I will work with this." Then there is also the "reactive" subject, who sees very well that something is happening but who prefers not to concern himself with this and even, if it is at all possible, that nobody concerns himself with the event, because he prefers the established laws of the world. And, finally, there is the "obscure" subject, who is the one who downright negates that anything has happened at all and who endeavors to destroy all fidelity as a myth, as something fallacious and detrimental. The reactive subject does not say that the event did not exist; he recognizes that perhaps something has happened, but he says: "It is better not to concern oneself with this." In politics, the differences are clear: the obscure subject, in particular, is deeply troubled by the existence of people who pretend that something has happened, and therefore this type of subject claims that nothing has happened at all. There you have, broadly speaking, the spectrum of three subjective possibilities in relation to the event.

IV. THE HISTORY OF PHILOSOPHY: FROM PLATO TO WITTGENSTEIN

> *Parmenides, Descartes, Spinoza, Kant, Hegel . . . The history of "classical" philosophy plays a very significant role in your work. Just now for example you spoke of Plato and you also pay your respects to him in your first* Manifesto for Philosophy. *Could you return to this issue by explaining in more detail why Plato is for you the first great philosopher?*

Concerning Plato as the first philosopher, I would say that he is the first complete philosopher, in the sense that he is the first philosopher truly to have placed the four conditions in relation to one another in a clear and systematic fashion. On the question of love, I have just quoted him:

Plato explains very well that whoever has never been in love cannot be a philosopher, and he devotes an entire dialogue, *The Symposium*, to this question. Incidentally, this dialogue goes very far, since it broaches the distinction between desire and love, and it develops the way in which an amorous truth is always a sublimation of sexuality, but not at all its disappearance. "Platonic love" is the name for this love in which, to put it crudely, people don't screw—which is a completely misleading definition, because this is not at all what Plato says. To the contrary, he speaks abundantly about desire, and the dialogue even revolves around the question of knowing whether Socrates is going to sleep with Alcibiades or not. Alcibiades indeed exudes a strong sexual attraction. So that is not where the problem is at; the problem rather consists in knowing what form the fidelity in love will take so that one may become witness to something that has a universal value, but that is not at all opposed to sexuality. The question is not about sexuality or no sexuality; the question is about love or passing fling, and thus ultimately about love or the simple game of desire. In other words, how can love include desire?

And then, of course, Plato also has submitted himself to the condition of mathematics. All that is well known. Some people even believe that he was an experienced mathematician of his time, when an important mutation took place, for example, with Eudoxus. I particularly admire how in his dialogue *Meno* he foregrounds the importance of mathematics in an exchange with a slave, someone from the lowest echelon of the social hierarchy, to show that this character at the bottom of the social ladder participates in the universality of which humanity is capable. Indeed, this slave will understand the proof of an extremely complicated theorem that was discovered at the time, a theorem that concerns the irrational character of the diagonal of the square. And this proof in a rather spectacular manner will show that we are dealing with an important truth destined for all of humanity. It is the only place in Plato's entire oeuvre where the slaves are mentioned. And it is striking to see that he talks about a slave only to show that the slave understands mathematics like everyone else. This is remarkable because it has political virtue in the large sense.

Plato has obviously concerned himself enormously with politics: politics was a great activity for the Greeks, and he actively sought to understand the sense of politics beyond democracy. Thus, he studied military oligarchy, then plutocracy and the world of the rich, and finally democracy. About democracy, he shows very well that it always ends in tyranny. And after having analyzed all that—which in fact are the political systems as they are normally determined in the world such as it is—he describes what I have called the "fifth politics," a form of politics to which he gives no other name. Incidentally, it is striking that this form of politics has no other name: it is politics itself, just that, politics as truth. And at the heart of this type of politics, what do we find? We find a radical concept of equality. To be sure, it is the equality among the guardians, so it is still an aristocratic equality, but that is not the crucial point. The crucial point is that Plato does not mention all the others. This is why what he says can easily be expanded to all the others. Exactly in the same way that one can broaden mathematics to include the slave, one can easily expand the definition of the guardians—which in some regards remains aristocratic—to everyone. What is the defining feature of the guardians? The fact that they own no private property. We should note that this is the first time in history that you have a philosophical polemic against private property as the source of corruption. On this basis, the norm obviously will be a norm of absolute equality. Besides, I should add in passing that Plato is often discussed by saying that his political doctrine is that of the philosopher-king, but this reference is totally absent from his work. We can find in this work a community of equals, and this community of equals is the model taken up in the nineteenth century by the burgeoning communist movement. We should recall that the different communist schools in the nineteenth century—whether utopian, Marxist, and so on—considered Plato a communist and the origin of communist thought.

We already talked about art: Plato is enmeshed in a constant interrogation regarding the problem of knowing what kind of poetry or theater are susceptible of being incorporated into the truth and whether this integration is desirable. This is because he nourishes the suspicion that the seduction of art perhaps is not really universal. In particular, he suspects the theater of aiming to maintain the existing affects. Theater would be a concession to the existing affects and therefore not a creation of a new universal affect. But this does not take away the fact that Plato submits himself to the artistic condition and engages in a never-ending dispute with this condition.

Thus, in my estimation, Plato is a perfect example of the systematic integration of the four conditions into his concept of the truth. He himself calls the truth an "Idea," but this falls under the paradigm of what he calls the Idea of the Good, which in fact is the Idea of the Idea. And this name covers the lesson he draws from his connection to the four conditions of philosophy.

> *You have written a very beautiful book on Wittgenstein under a peculiar title:* Wittgenstein's Antiphilosophy. *Could you explain this "antiphilosophy" a bit more, precisely with the help of Wittgenstein's figure?*

As a backdrop and by way of preamble, remember that philosophy is defined by a stance on the question of truths and that, by the same token, there always comes a moment when one must consider philosophically the negative positions, for which I reserve the term "antiphilosophy." However, I have always maintained that antiphilosophy is situated *within* philosophy, because the affirmative philosopher draws very interesting lessons from antiphilosophy itself.

Wittgenstein in his own way is a very interesting thinker, because he attempts to build a philosophy that would be centered not so much on a relationship to the conditions of truth but on a relationship to what we can call the language situations. He is the one who introduces, or one of the first introducers, of an idea that will have a very important career in the twentieth century: namely, the idea that philosophy ultimately is the attempt to find a correct language, to find a language that would not be deceiving. Thus, some element of truth continues to circulate a little bit in this way in Wittgenstein's case, since he is simply going to displace the issue by arguing that ultimately the question is that of sense and nonsense, rather than that of true and false. For him, what one has called true is not something that is clear, and there is only what makes sense and what does not make sense. Thus, he considers that practically everything that has been told in philosophy until him is nonsense. But that, in the end, is the arrogance of the philosophers, and he has not been the only one to be like this.

Therefore, Wittgenstein launches himself into an exploration that should enable him to delimit what makes sense and what does not make sense. The problem is that making sense or not making sense does not delimit any immanent exceptions in the way that I talk about them. There is no direct relationship to my category of truth. It would rather be an attempt to undo the idea of truth and replace it with the idea of sense as the only hope that would be possible relatively speaking for thought today. This devaluation of the truth to the benefit of sense is perhaps after all a philosophical option, but in my view it is antiphilosophical, because I define philosophy as centered on being, truth, and subject. For this reason I would situate Wittgenstein, like all those who privilege sense over the truth, on the side of those I call antiphilosophers. And from this point of view there is a paradoxical similarity between Wittgenstein and Nietzsche.

In modernity, these antiphilosophical figures gain much importance because paradoxically they have benefited from the complicity with the academic view of philosophy. This is a topic to which one day I would have liked to consecrate a short essay. How is it possible that people like Nietzsche or Wittgenstein—who were rebels and who presented themselves as people who destroyed the established traditions, and for whom the vital sense of things was more important than the fake sense—how is it possible that these very people have been annexed so easily, philosophically speaking, by the apparatus of the academy? To the point of becoming, like Wittgenstein, the great star of the whole American academic philosophy? There are good reasons for this, and yet at the same time it is based on a misunderstanding. Indeed, I think that the Wittgenstein of American analytical philosophy is certainly a Wittgenstein kept in a tin can, a dried up, pickled, and presentable Wittgenstein. Especially if we consider that Wittgenstein was some odd character. We should recall that he was a partisan of the Soviet Union, that he was a homosexual who was almost out of the closet . . . So he was not at all a character who would be easily presentable in a normal American university at the time. Nor was Nietzsche, frankly. As for me, I love Wittgenstein and Nietzsche a lot, I wrote an entire seminar on each one of them, but it must be said that they were nonetheless extravagant figures. Nietzsche ended up with a formula that in my view should be the subject of meditation for all professors, since he declared: "Finally, my life has been that I preferred becoming a professor in Basel rather than being God." One tries to imagine an honorable professor at an American university saying: "You know, my drama is that I preferred being your professor rather than God!"

Nietzsche, Wittgenstein, Kierkegaard, Lacan . . . When one considers these antiphilosophers, it is striking to see how they lead us in the direction of the history of modern philosophy.

In effect, I think that the history of philosophy begins with Plato, under the sign of the systematic elaboration of the conditions, of the relation to the conditions, of the creation of a great many concepts that will have a long posterity (being, thinking, the Idea, truth, all this with reference to the system of the conditions). And this history has continued through various twists and turns, and at the opposite end, on the cusp of the twentieth century, one finds several specifically modern antiphilosophical currents. I think this is because something in the very nature of philosophy properly speaking has been affected, altered, or rendered difficult in the passage to the twentieth century.

What exactly are we talking about? It is not as simple as that, but I think that philosophy has had the feeling, justifiably so, of not being up to par with the giant events that have marked the twentieth century—that it has had the feeling that its categories did not manage to grasp, for example, the massacre of millions of people during the war of 1914. What exactly was the Bolshevik Revolution, and then Stalin? What exactly was fascism? And above all, what was the Neolithic world that led to the unleashing of technology? In this regard I agree with Heidegger on the question of the nihilist element swept along with the capitalist predation, which has all the weaponry needed for this purpose at its disposal and colonizes all the technological inventions. I think that if there is one big question, this is it. Marx and many others already had broached this question in the nineteenth century, but it is still there. And faced with this question, philosophy has found itself a bit at a loss.

V. "CHANGING THE WORLD" / "CORRUPTING THE YOUTH"

All thinking is thus always situated—a thinking at a moment in time, a thinking of the time, of the times, including the times of crisis. Here is another question that plays a major role in your work: how to change the world from a philosophical point of view? And above all, why change the world?

Everything is connected, because the figure of Heidegger is at the very least symptomatic from this point of view. Heidegger indeed thinks that this nihilist situation has somehow come about by accompanying philosophy in its disappearance. And for him the evil started as early as Plato, and things were better before that. I absolutely disagree with this position, but I understand very well what Heidegger means when he speaks of a crisis. This is also Husserl's vocabulary, and finally today this is everybody's vocabulary: everybody thinks there is a crisis. Is philosophy capable of seizing hold of this crisis, while maintaining its fundamental aims? That is obviously my position. I certainly recognize that humanity is in crisis, which I take to be the final spasm of the whole Neolithic period, the period of classes, of private property, of the power of the state, of technology, and so on. This started in Egypt and China six or seven thousand years ago and now this ends up in what is after all a very difficult situation to control. It is the outcome of everything that this gigantic period has swept along with it. This includes the status of truths, which today are perhaps a bit domesticated by an uncontrollable situation of predation and destruction.

After all, technology is tributary to science; everything is supposed to be mediated by information, even aesthetics; love has become calculable because you can calculate scientifically the person who best matches with you. All this indeed is at the origin of a gigantic crisis in philosophy. My own position is that we can be in a position of active resistance to what is happening, while holding onto the original categories of philosophy. A form of resistance that nevertheless consists in dramatically changing into something else. We should not hope to reform the world such as it is: I think this is completely impossible. Of course, one can try to do the best one can, but little by little everyone recognizes that the world we live in is catastrophic. And that is certainly true. It is catastrophic because it is the end—and here we should think big—of several millennia. It is not just the end of the nineteenth and twentieth centuries; it is the end of the world of social classes, of inequalities, of state power, of the subservience to science and technology, of private property colonizing everything, of senseless and criminal wars.

This worldwide context also has been that of the most remarkable invention of truths in the system of the four conditions. Our problem therefore is that this world has witnessed the birth and development of the conditions of philosophy, as well as of philosophy itself, and this is a world that is also in a certain sense the annihilation of all that, or of its nihilistic use. Philosophy is in crisis, this much is evident. What would be fatal, however, is if we were to abandon it. That would be an invitation for the final abandonment. Philosophy must give an account of all that, and it must do so according to the general system of the conditions. And here it is obviously the question of the political commitment of the philosopher today that is inevitable. I think that despite everything, from this point of view, we come back to the figure of the committed philosopher, because we are forced to. Academic philosophy serves absolutely no purpose. My old master Sartre said "We do not deserve our true ancestors." And when people would ask him "But who are our true ancestors?" he answered "Rousseau, Voltaire, and the *philosophes* of the French Revolution." I think that he was right: today we must reestablish this type of status that makes philosophy on the one hand speculative, conceptual, devoted to the truths, under certain conditions, and, on the other hand, precisely because it is all that, philosophy must take on the role of radical commitment against the contemporary world in its dominant form.

> *We thus come back to the beginnings of philosophy, to Socrates and therefore to Plato, because you are one of the rare philosophers who is committed to addressing himself directly to the youth. How, in the footsteps of Socrates, can one "corrupt the youth"?*

I think that today the youth is exposed to all the risks of the world that we have described just a moment ago—that is, a world in which finally humanity's predatory activity has become catastrophic. "To corrupt the youth," thus, means to give them the means to disengage themselves and throw themselves into the pursuit of a way out of all this. We know that there are a certain number of tendencies that go in this direction, but the youth is also, if I may say so, in part and very early on corrupted by the figures of the contemporary world.

Lenin said that the youth is always a "sensitive plate" of its time, and I believe that as an image this is right on the mark. The youth is a sensitive plate in a double sense. Firstly, its sensibility is shaped by the world such as it is, and then secondly, it is capable of sensing very vividly the malfeasance or the mediocrity or the evil side of this world. And what the philosopher can do is to corrupt the youth, to tear it away from its interiority to the world such as it is. This is exactly what Socrates was reproached for and earned him the death sentence: to give the youth the theoretical, formal, and conceptual tools to support the positive tendencies that may exist in it, that is, those tendencies that go in the direction of an exit from the world as it is. We must encourage this to fight against the youth's spontaneous adherence to contemporary nihilism. For me, to corrupt the youth means to extricate it from nihilism, which is a form of adhesion to the decomposed character of the contemporary world. And I think that an organization of philosophy that refers truly to the complete system of the four conditions can draw up the balance sheet of this era in a clear and convincing way for the youth. Today, in any case, philosophy as I conceive of it can truly play its role in close proximity to the youth.

Let us recall that Socrates and Plato were people who already intervened at the end of the Greek city. They too found themselves in a world threatened by catastrophe: they did not live in a stable and established world at all. That ends with Alexander the Great, who brings order to all this in the form of an imperial creation, and finally with the Romans and their monster of a state the likes of which had never been seen before. The Greek city and Greek democracy thus ended in the imperialism of ancient Rome. Thus, we may also find inspiration in Plato in this last regard. Plato is the first complete philosopher, but he already lives in a time of crisis. Of course, Athens was very famous and celebrated, but at the same time it was already corrupted and fragile. During Plato's own lifetime, not to mention Aristotle, Macedonian imperialism is already present. Aristotle was Alexander the Great's first tutor; he was a prototype of the corrupted and, moreover, the inventor of academic philosophy!

Similarly, if we take the greatest philosophers—Plato, Descartes, Hegel—we again find the same type of figure. Hegel is obviously the philosopher caught up in the French Revolution and its fundamental transformations; Descartes, for his part, is caught up in the emergence of modern science. All these philosophers are caught up in considerable shakeups of their time, in the fact that an old society is on the verge of dying and the question of what is going to appear that is new. We too find ourselves in the same situation: we must continue along these lines, by taking inspiration from what those philosophers did. Thus, they considered that the moment had come to work on a renewed systematicity of philosophy, because the conditions had changed. So, based on the conditions as they existed, it was time to propose an innovative way out of the existing constraints, an individual and collective liberation. From this point of view, we can find inspiration in the great classical philosophical tradition: we need not reject it, nor claim that all this is finished and find solace in an insurmountable nihilism, nor adopt the Heideggerian critique of metaphysics going back all the way to Plato. All this is pointless, and finally becomes incorporated into the disorder of the world. On the contrary, we must hold onto the fact that philosophy has always been particularly useful, possible, and necessary in situations of grave crisis for the collective, and from there pursue the work of our great predecessors.

VI. EQUALITY, UNIVERSALITY, EMANCIPATION: THE COMMUNIST IDEA

There are a great many commentators who do not wish to understand the importance of communism—that is, the communist idea or hypothesis—for your thinking. Nevertheless, it is an idea closely linked to equality, universality, and a politics of emancipation. Could you try once more to explain to them the importance of this idea?

If we restart from the previous question and place ourselves for an instant under the condition of politics in the broad sense, we will observe on the one hand that the situation is one of crisis and decomposition, and on the other hand that, in the logic of its emergence in the nineteenth century, "communism" is the name given to the way out from all this: the way out from the subservience of the system of philosophy's conditions to something aimed at their destruction. Thus, to love, one opposes calculable enjoyment; to politics, a simple system for the management of the dominant forces; to art, the supposedly universal appeal of communication; and to science, technology. "Communism" means or designates the will to exit from all that and affirm the priority of the common over private interest, which is also, when we transpose this onto the philosophical domain strictly speaking, the affirmation of the superiority of truths over opinions. I think we can put it this way.

In a first sense, "communism" is thus a generic name. It turns out, furthermore, that this was the name for a specific political endeavor, invented and formulated by Marx, but also by the various utopian communists of the nineteenth century, then implemented starting with the Bolshevik Revolution of 1917 in the guise of several states. Except that we must immediately recall that "communist state" is a paradox, a contradiction. This is why after Lenin, who had insisted on this point, people have taken the precaution of speaking only of a socialist state and maintained the idea that communism meant the withering away, or the end, of the state. And as we know, instead of obtaining the end of the state, unfortunately we have seen its constant reinforcement in truly tyrannical conditions.

We therefore must draw up the balance sheet of all that. But it would be false and very perilous to draw up this balance sheet while abandoning the word "communism." On the contrary, we must hold up the thesis that the word "communism" has been corrupted by the power of the state. That is the truth. It is false to say that the Russian and Chinese Revolutions have accomplished nothing. They have accomplished a great many things—we therefore ought not to reject them as if they had been nothing but despotism. We should recognize that they transformed the lives of millions of people, putting into relief the dignity of workers and peasants in contexts where they were despised to the highest degree; they relaunched an educational system that has proven itself to be excellent after all; they created a health system that did not exist, etc. That being said, globally, it is true that the communist idea has become corrupted by the exercise of state power. In passing I wish to indicate that Lenin had seen all this already in the 1920s. In this regard we have texts at our disposal that show him being extremely anxious and full of doubt: he goes so far as to say that, all in all, the Bolshevik state was worth no more than the Tsarist state. He wrote this as clear as black and white in the 1920s. This corruption of communism—which at the beginning was the idea of the exit from the Neolithic period, exit from the six thousand years that preceded it—shows up very early on. A result of this certainly has been a slightly different state formation, but one that was able to sustain itself only at the cost of enormous despotic effort.

On the contrary, to struggle against the disastrous effects of this corruption—that is, the failure of this first attempt—we must absolutely maintain and reactivate the word "communism." If we abandon it, we will end up being defenseless, because we will not be able to designate what is at stake. We will not inscribe ourselves in this trajectory, which started in the nineteenth century and even a bit before that—since the communist ideas already show up in Rousseau—and which continues to this day. There is no reason whatsoever to abandon this tradition under the pretext that at a given moment it attempted to pull off an experiment that failed. There have always been failures, and there will be others, but that is not our tribunal. Our tribunal is the maintenance of the vigor of the orientation in question, and of its resurrection based on the state of weakness in which it finds itself today.

Finally, the tasks of the new communism—let us call it thus to distinguish it from the old—are philosophically clear: we must reactivate the central character of the egalitarian dimension that was at the core of the communist proposition. We must constantly recall that this egalitarian dimension of society must accompany a progressive withering away of the state, and that it is not compatible with the indefinite maintenance and reinforcement of a central power that is practically cut off from the ensemble of people's lives. The latter is totally contrary to the communist idea.

In addition, we must realize that the principles of communism are not at all reducible to the nationalization of private property and production. In fact, it is even possible to have reactionary nationalizations: during the financial crisis of 2008, we have seen the American government nationalize the banks, which proves that "nationalization" is an equivocal term. In fact, nationalization is formal, or juridical, whereas what is at stake is the collective appropriation of the means of production. At the end of his life,

Mao went so far as to ask the question: let us assume that the factories have been nationalized; but does this mean our factories are *really* different from the capitalist factories?

I have always been tempted to formalize this by saying that there were four great principles of communism, such as I see it in its strategic aim and such as philosophy is capable of speaking about it under the condition of real experiences. The first principle is in effect the collective appropriation of the means of production and finance. However, let us remember that collective appropriation and nationalization do not mean the same thing: we must invent the collective appropriation in the context of nationalization. The second principle is that we must put an end to the absolute necessity of the hierarchical division of labor: we must treat and reduce the differences between manual labor and intellectual labor, between the work of management and the work of production, between the post of command and the post of execution. Normally these differences must be reduced, and we thus need an effective politics for their reduction and their disappearance. The third principle is that the world space must be internationalist in the strong sense. Marx's formula on this topic was radical—"the proletariat has no fatherland"—after which, on the contrary, we have witnessed the appearance of the expression "the USSR is the fatherland of socialism," which is totally contradictory. Internationalism thus must be reinvented. And the experiment that one can propose to the youth for the reinvention of this internationalism is to intervene on the question of migrations in a way that is radically opposed to the dominant logic, which furthermore, when it is fully deployed, turns out to be slightly fascistic. Finally, the fourth principle is that all this must be done by way of collective decision-making procedures that would be less and less state-like, authoritarian, and centralized. That is the process of the withering away of the state.

If we speak of communism, we therefore must say all the above. If we do not, then one does not understand anything about communism. And if we do say all that, then we can understand why the experiment has failed: the first point has been addressed, but practically none of the others.

PART TWO

Philosophy Between Mathematics and Poetry

WE WILL BEGIN with a few very general considerations about philosophy as such. You know that Socrates was condemned to death because he had been accused of "corrupting the youth." We must assume this accusation. Yes, philosophy corrupts the youth and ultimately it corrupts everyone. Philosophy organizes a series of ruptures, an opening onto a new life, a true life as opposed to the fallacious life that the capitalist market and the cult of money propose to us.

To clarify the stakes and the means of philosophy, we will concentrate on the conditions of philosophy, which are defined by the relation between philosophy and four different forms of truth: scientific, artistic, amorous, and political. We will examine more specifically how philosophy, with all the complexity characteristic of philosophical language, is caught between mathematics and poetry, between the rigorous construction of arguments and the seduction of language.

Thesis 1.

Mathematical proofs and rational philosophy are born at the same time in the same place, namely, in Greece in the fifth century before the common era. Philosophy is born in Greece under the condition of mathematics but in the language of poetry. From this point onward, philosophy has always been dominated by a certain tension between its demonstrative or mathematical tendency and its seductive or poetic tendency. You thus have Spinoza on the one hand and Nietzsche on the other.

Thesis 2.

This tension has sometimes taken the form of a conflict or a contradiction. Thus, Plato spoke of a "very old quarrel between poetry and philosophy." For his part, he violently attacked poetry, even if he often declared his love for it. This conflict is not so much objective (in the sense of the difference between various types of languages) as it is subjective. Poetry and philosophy both have attempted to produce, solely through their language, two different forms of converting their audience. Philosophy's ambition is to replace the authoritarian discourse with an argumentative discourse. Indeed, a statement is true not because it has been pronounced by a priest, a king, a prophet, or a god. It is true because there is proof of its truth. Thus, every supposed truth must be able to be submitted to a general discussion, and the subject of the enunciation ought not be the guarantor of the truth of a statement. It is the statements that have already been guaranteed as true that constitute the proof of the truth of a new statement. Poetry, for its part, is much more situated on the side of seduction, of subjective transformation, which is produced with the force and beauty of language as such.

Thesis 3.
The difficulty is precisely that, before Socrates, philosophy emerged in a language that was still poetic, largely inspired by Homer's long poems. As a result, it was closer to poetry than to mathematics. This was the time of Empedocles and Anaximander. The transition took place in the work of Parmenides: he too wrote a long poem. But in fact he proposed a proof, the logical proof that only being is, thus placing philosophy between poetry and mathematics. To prove that only being is and nothing else, he had recourse to the indirect method of reasoning from the absurd. In fact, he has tried to demonstrate that non-being cannot exist and, consequently, only being exists. The fact that non-being does not exist seems evident, but we must understand that for Parmenides "being" and "existing" are two different things.

In any case, beginning with Parmenides, philosophy is situated between poetry and mathematics, and Plato takes it upon himself to continue in this demonstrative manner, without sacrificing anything whatsoever in terms of the beauty of language. In fact, the genre of poetry that Plato criticizes is not poetry in general but poetry that he calls "mimetic," namely, that which places itself under the pressure of a natural model, whose aim is not to create new knowledge but a new affect. For Plato the models of this "bad" poetry are the epic poems on the one hand, and, on the other hand and above all, the tragic theater. So it is less a question of language than a question of the subjective effects produced by poetry, insofar as an uncontrolled seduction allows the spectators and listeners to identify themselves with models of thoughts, sentiments, and actions, which is unacceptable for the philosopher. We must admit that in the end Plato is not opposed to poetry as such. He accepts poetry on the condition that it not be mimetic. His fundamental argument is that philosophy is the creation of something and not the imitation of something.

Finally, after Parmenides the language of philosophy is situated mid-way between poetic language and mathematical language. You could say that there is a language of seduction or a seductive power, which produces a transference onto the speaking person, and a language of proof, which reduces the listener to silence.

Thesis 4.
Plato himself constantly makes poetic use of language, particularly in the form of "myths," which are a kind of fable that produces and modifies the concepts by inventing a fictional approach to their origin and their history.

As opposed to poetic stories, fables, or, briefly put, fictional language, the force of mathematics consists in relying on symbols, letters, figures, or formulae rather than on words, images, or phrases. Here is an example of mathematical language:

$$[\forall y \, (y \notin x)] \leftrightarrow (x = \emptyset)$$

This formula means: "to affirm that, for every set y, it is not true that y belongs to x, is equivalent to saying that x is the empty set." We can say that mathematics proves the power of the letter, of pure letters and symbols, of pure demonstration or symbolization, whereas poetry is the power of language, of discourse, of its images and its development.

Thesis 5.

Precisely for this reason, there has never been any philosophy written entirely in mathematical language, for philosophy, even when it is demonstrative, has never reached this level of formalization. The dream or idea of a purely mathematical philosophy, which would be written exclusively with letters and symbols and in which all sentences would be theorems, is impossible. Spinoza represents the extreme case, having written his famous book *Ethics* in the form of Euclid's great treatise. But even Spinoza is very far from a rigorous symbolization. It is even possible to affirm that finally Spinoza's *Ethics* propose a kind of abstract poetry. Besides, there are philosophical works that explicitly present themselves in poetic form, such as Lucretius *De rerum natura* or certain parts of Nietzsche's *Thus Spoke Zarathustra*.

We can conclude from this that philosophy does not permit the pure power of the letter. It needs the meaning of words. It certainly may attempt to be demonstrative, but it cannot be entirely formalized. This is why philosophy is situated between mathematics and poetry.

Thesis 6.

Mathematics, as the formal ontology of multiplicities, is an independent science that constitutes a closed field. Poetry, on the other hand, as an extraordinary treatment of ordinary language, may emerge from any text whatsoever.

Moreover, mathematics is written in a single language, whereas poetry is written in numerous languages, which raises the question of how the universality of philosophy is possible. Indeed, from the very beginning philosophers have affirmed that what they thought or wrote had universal value. In this sense, a philosopher proposes something universal beyond the national languages or through the differences among existing languages. And mathematics could precisely represent a universal language of this kind, since it finds support in the power of the letter. However, we saw that for the writings of philosophy, the letter is not enough. This is a difficult problem because if philosophy is by necessity written in a national language, its universality will be proven or controlled by the translations. We thus must suppose that in the case of philosophy there are translations that do not present real transformations or modifications of its universal signification. This point raises the delicate question of the relation between philosophy and translation.

Thesis 7.
Philosophy can and must raise the question of knowing why mathematics, in its formalization, is used in all the natural sciences, especially in physics, which deals with the concrete objects and laws of nature. I will answer that this stems from the fact that mathematics is the science of all that is—not insofar as it is this or that, but insofar as it is.

From the point of view of philosophy, mathematics constitutes the demonstrative apparatus of all the thinking of being, the thought of being qua being, of what is insofar as it is (it is neither a tree nor a person). This begins with Parmenides, for whom being is being, since non-being is not. Seen from the same point of view, poetry constitutes, within language, the capacity to seize the event. In this sense, my own philosophy stands in relation to poetry, not from the side of being, of what is, but from the side of the event, of what happens and is not immediately identifiable with what is. Think for instance of artistic creations (which are creations of something that is not already there) or of love (which is what happens or not), or of scientific inventions that turn all previous knowledge upside down.

Thesis 8.
The common feature of everything is that everything is multiple. Nothing in nature is in itself absolutely one. Again, from the point of view of mathematics, everything that is constitutes a form of multiplicity. Nothing in nature is absolutely one; this water bottle, for example, is composed of multiple things. To be is to be multiple, and mathematics is the science of the multiple. The question of mathematics in philosophy is therefore the question of multiplicity. In other words, to think of the multiple in its purest form is as an object for mathematics, whereas to think of the multiple in philosophy is sometimes complex, sometimes simple (which explains why mathematics can be useful for philosophy). Perhaps God is the sole exception. If He exists, God is absolutely One. Whence the importance of God in philosophy: metaphysics treats the absolute One in the form of God, the great One, as opposed to us, since we are multiplicities. Everything that is natural, or material, is composed of elements that are equally natural or material.

This gives us a fundamental choice between an ontology of the One and an ontology of the multiple. Think for example of the history of philosophy and of the numerous attempts to prove the existence of God (for example, in Descartes or Leibniz). In the philosophical sense, God is not on the order of affect, of belief, but stands in relation to a proof as to the necessity of the great infinite-One. The mathematical side is important to the extent that we speak of the conflict between a rational proof, from the point of view of philosophy, for the existence of the One, on the one hand, and a mathematical ontology that treats all possible forms of the multiple, on the other.

Poetry, for its part, attests to the power of the spirit to force language to say what is impossible to say. From the point of view of philosophy, the existence of this power allows us to say that truths are universal, because they are founded on events. This means that they go beyond the ontological laws of the worlds in which they appear.

Poetry for me is the possibility of thinking what happens: the pure event. An event by force is what happens and subsequently disappears. This is why I think it is necessary to move from the classical view of the One (God as the great One) to the thought of the pure multiple and the difficulty there is in thinking the new. The history of philosophy then becomes the history of the changeover it proposes with regard to the fundamental questions. The old metaphysics in general considers what is by regarding what is not, or of the One as opposed to the multiple, or, again, of the infinity of God detaching itself from the finitude of the sensible. Today, I think that one fundamental question concerns the gap between being (what is) and the event (what happens). That, in any case, as it always happens in philosophy, is my personal choice. The philosopher always takes on the task of realizing a program whose point of departure constitutes a network of questions that he or she has chosen.

Thesis 9.
There are only two possible sciences of being. If you think that God exists, there must be a science of the forms of the One, which is called theology. Otherwise, there is only

the science of all the possible forms of the multiple. This is ontology.

Escaping all the forms of ontology, each poem is the name of an event. Here is an example that comes to us from the French poet Paul Valéry. The title of the poem is "To the Plantain Tree." It is the story of an attempt to enclose the great tree within the image of a pure object in the landscape and its site, and thus not assigned to an event but to the peaceful force of the world as it is:

> You lean, great Plantain, and offer yourself naked,
> > Pale as a young Scythe
> But your candor is caught, and your foot held back
> > By the force of the site.

You see how the tree becomes a victim of sorts of its own beauty, prisoner to the site. We are witnesses to its pure objectivization.

However, at the end of the poem, you have the revolt of the tree against this objectivization. The tree wishes to be, not a splendid prisoner, but part of an event, of a violent event, a tempest. And it replies: "No, I do not accept becoming simply a piece of a structure."

> No, says the tree, it says "No" with the sparkling
> > Of its superb head,
> That the tempest treats universally
> > Just as it does with a leaf of grass!

Thesis 10.
Ontology is integrally thinkable only in the language and logic of mathematics. This science can make use of the power of the letter, for letters do not concern the meaning

of what is or the law of what is. Their only purpose is to serve to annotate, reflect, and classify the possible forms of what is, as well as the possible relation between these forms. Mathematics can be literal, because it does not concern what is singular, but only the universality of the forms adopted by singularities.

Philosophy, which thinks of truths as a mixture of being and event, is a kind of poeticization of mathematics.

Thesis 11.
Mathematics can be used to formulate the laws of nature, because all the singular objects of nature are equally and mainly parts of what is insofar as it is. Every object that exists is in the possible form of a multiplicity. This is why mathematics thinks and formulates the ontological basis of physics.

In the nineteenth century and during a large part of the twentieth, the dominance of positivism (and thus of science), on the one hand, and on the other, of history (and thus of politics) has had the effect of creating an age of the poets that goes from Hölderlin to Paul Celan and includes Rimbaud, Mallarmé, Trakl, Mandelstam, Pessoa, Stevens, Vallejo, and a few others. During this whole period, poetry assumed the tasks that ordinarily are those of philosophy, particularly: to think everything that belongs to the unpredictable, to the impossible, to the functioning of chance, and the new figures of heroism.

Thesis 12.
Philosophy must situate itself beyond theology, which is the religious science of the forms of the One, but also beyond pure ontology, which is the secular science of the forms of

the multiple (mathematics). Philosophy begins when it is a question of thinking not only what is, but the being of what is not, and the effect of what is not on what is. Philosophy therefore must think the event and clarify the importance of what happens and disappears. All this is not reducible to the form of multiplicity. An event is an event within a concrete context, and because of this it is by nature poetic. Therefore, philosophy must know what happens in the field of poetry. This also explains the very close relation between poetry and love, with the latter being the principal example of what happens that is universal and creative in a human life.

In the final years of the twentieth century, the failure of the second period of communism (that of the socialist states) and the crisis in the sciences (abandoned to commercial interests) have restored the independence of philosophy and put an end to the age of the poets.

Thesis 13.
Philosophy must recognize with great precision the ontology that is mathematics. It has a duty to understand all the possible forms of the multiple, and especially the profound mathematical theories of the modern era about the different types of infinities. However, philosophy is the thinking not only of what is, but also of what happens to what is: not only of being, but also of the event; not only of the forms of the possible, but also of the re-forming into something new what, at a given moment, is considered impossible. That is why, today more than ever, there can be no philosophy worthy of its name without a meditation on the work of the poets, in particular those prodigious poets of the age of the poets.

Philosophy is a meditation regarding the existence of truths that result from the event in a given situation of being. A truth is something new, because it is also a construction composed, on the one hand, of pure multiplicities that belong to a situation, and on the other hand, of an event that happens in the situation. This relation is crucial: the result of the event is the realization, within the order of being, of the process that brings forth the appearance of a new truth, the creation of the truth in the framework of its four conditions (science, art, love, and politics). Philosophy thus situates itself between poetry (what happens, the event) and mathematics (what is, being).

PART THREE

Ontology and Mathematics

I. PHILOSOPHY AND ITS CONDITIONS

As several of you know, for me philosophy exists as long as there are truth procedures, and it is conditioned by the historical state of these procedures. I have arranged the truths of which humankind has proven itself capable, over the course of thousands of years of existence, into four great types: the sciences, the arts, politics, and love.

The question then becomes how we may interrogate, throughout the history of philosophy, the link between philosophy and its conditions. The difficulty, which I would like to summarize here, is that we must consider three different approaches in the investigation of the historical corpus of philosophy that we have inherited.

The first approach is to consider, at every moment in the history of philosophy, *the state of the four conditions and their impact on philosophy in a determinate place.* This is the panoramic view, which is essentially historiographical. It allows us to distinguish, with more or less efficiency, certain philosophical epochs or territories. Thus, we speak of "ancient philosophy" or "medieval philosophy," or again "continental philosophy" as opposed to "analytical philosophy," mainly in the United States.

The second process is attached to *staking out a problem, internal to one condition, which modifies the whole prior relation of philosophy to the array of its conditions.* This is evidently the case of the mathematical mutation provoked in the fifth century before the common era by the discovery of "incommensurable" lengths, which tilts Greek mathematics from Pythagorean arithmetic toward the geometry of Eudoxus and Euclid; and, in philosophy, from the search for Harmony to a theory of ruptures. We could also invoke the political effects of the French Revolution, which forces German philosophy, beginning with Fichte, to make profound dialectical reformulations that bring to light the creative force of negativity.

The third approach resides in the possibility that a philosophy—and, thus, in the first place, a philosopher—may intervene from the point of view of philosophy itself in the dynamic of at least one of the four conditions. This is *the retroactive process, from philosophy back onto the conditions.* There is no doubt, for example, that Platonism in the long run has influenced the social vision of love in the era of its courtly spiritualization, or that the Hegelian dialectic has had a constitutive influence on communist politics as founded by Marx. Or again, we could trace the influence of the materialist and libertine philosophy, derived from Epicurus, in the theatrical work of Molière and a few others.

All this should remind us of the fact that the word "condition" is different from the word "cause." Finally, with the arts, the sciences, politics, love, and philosophy, what is at stake are five intertwined processes, even if we must continue to be clear about the fact that philosophy occupies the singular position of not being able to exist without the other four, whereas they can exist by themselves.

II. "IN THE SITUATION"

When thirty years ago I launched, as one does in politics with a watchword, the formula "ontology = mathematics," I had no doubt about its potential success, but I did not correctly anticipate its drawbacks. Indeed, all in all, the formula has the advantage of being striking but the inconvenience of being approximate. By relating in a somewhat brutal and identitarian fashion a typically philosophical concept, that of ontology, to the disposition of a particular science, mathematics, the formula fails to take fully into account the complex nature of the relations between philosophy and its conditions. I will return, therefore, to the relation between mathematics and philosophy on the basis of my introductory considerations.

Let us start out from the first of the three processes or approaches that I defined in my previous section—namely, the global history of the quartet of conditions. How did these four conditions, such as they presented themselves to me in France some fifty years ago, become operative in the philosophical field? What inventions, what creations, what problems drew my attention in this context?

1. In the development of mathematics, it is the work of Paul Cantor, with the theory of *forcing* and the concept of the *generic set* that overhauls set theory, even in relation to Gödel's genial inventions in the 1930s and 1940s. It is also the veritable breakthrough of the *theory of categories*,

Ontology and Mathematics 51

which in the mathematical field tends to replace the notion of object with that of relation.

2. In politics, we have the contrasting balance sheet of the vast mass movements that energized the student youth and the working class, almost everywhere in the world, during the 1960s and 1970s—notably May 1968 in France and the Great Proletarian Cultural Revolution in China. This balance sheet finally is overshadowed by the global failure of these movements—a failure that accompanies the bankruptcy of the socialist states, Russia and China included, as well as the lessons that communists must draw from this bankruptcy.

3. In the arts, the most consistent and lasting novelty can be found in the plastic arts, with *performances*, which turn the artists' body into a decisive element of their work, and *installations*, which register the provisory and local dimension of spatial structures. In both cases, it is a question of rendering every aesthetic disposition provisory, of relativizing the work of art in time and space and thus to put an end to the idea that the work of art would have an objective and eternal value.

4. In love, the new social freedom in sexuality, the crisis of familial authorities, the emancipation of women, the legalization of contraceptive measures, the promotion of a festive vision of existence, the autonomization of simple desire as a right to be vindicated: all this converges toward a precarization of the amorous bond, even—with the "dating sites"—toward a kind of commercial calculus as to its value and its eventual application. However, a wholly different take is involved in Lacan's reworking of the psychoanalytical point of view, with the famous

formula "Being is what love comes to approach in the encounter," which turns love into the possible location of an ontology of the subject.

When looked at in detail, the conditioning materials lead rather naturally, in the order of what presents itself as "philosophy," to two types of consequences. On the one hand, we find a cultural relativism that leaves no more room for the notion of universal truth, taken to be an imperialist fiction, and privileges the multiplicity of languages and customs, the planetary colorings as well as the multiple forms of identities, which are systematically preferred over and above all great constructions with a global aim. On the other hand, we find doctrines that affirm the superiority of actions over thoughts, of movement over organization, of intuition over the Idea, of life over structures, of the local approach over the value of the global, of complex multiplicities over the dialectical dualism, of affirmation over negativity—in short, doctrines that, against Plato, Descartes, or Hegel, return to the Stoics, Hume, or Nietzsche, which is accomplished to perfection in Deleuze.

And yet, it is based on these same materials "in the situation" that my properly philosophical desire discerns the essential task of reconstructing, against the two tendencies that spontaneously appear to be dominant and, moreover, complicitous with each other: a speculative discursivity capable of organizing anew those questions that the dominant currents separate from their becoming, namely, the questions of being, of truth, and of the subject. And since we started with ontology, let us begin there.

III. ONTOLOGIES

If I consider my thinking on being qua being in the context of the history of this question, I believe it is possible to distinguish it from no less than six possibilities as to what finally has been called "ontology."

First, two positions that are ultimately negative

1. The concept of being is empty, having no meaning whatsoever. This is the dominant view today, for the reasons I just enumerated. It is always the skeptical position. It is also the positivist position, as we can see in the case of Auguste Comte. It is the explicit position of the vitalists. It is also the position of Wittgenstein and of the entire analytical current in the United States. For all these thinkers, the word "being" is in fact an illegitimate substantivization of the verb "to be this or that," a substantivization that produces a pure non-sense.

2. The concept of being has a sense, it has a positive value. But we cannot obtain any effective knowledge of its content. The "thing in itself" is situated beyond our cognitive faculties. As is well known, this is Kant's position, but finally it is the "being-historical" position of Heidegger: contemporary nihilism, linked to the sovereign violence of technology, leads us not only (as in all metaphysics since Plato) to forget the true meaning of being, its destiny, but we also have forgotten this forgetting itself. We thus have become completely estranged not only from the meaning of being, but even from the question of meaning, which nonetheless constitutes us in the history of being.

Then, four positive positions

All these positions affirm that the word "being" has a real meaning and that we can have a true, grounded knowledge of this meaning. But this first affirmation subsequently distributes itself into essentially different, and even opposite, orientations.

1. The third position opens the path to the different forms of monotheism: being gives itself, in an explicit and concentrated manner, in the form of the One, the great One, or the One as Infinite. This is by and large the position of classical metaphysics, which Heidegger was not wrong to define as the "enframing of Being by the One." In fact, this is already Aristotle's position, for whom being is exhibited as "pure actuality" in the transcendence of a god. And the path of the donation of the meaning of being in his case takes the philosophical form, which for a long time will be dominant, of a *proof* of the existence of the One-of-being as such. At the same time, you will find the mystical current for which the access to the transcendence of being is a vital experience, and not a proof—an experience whose story is poetic rather than logico-mathematical. This current belongs to the artistic condition, as we can see with Saint John of the Cross, and not to the scientific condition, as for example in Malebranche. But in both cases, life-thought gains access to being only in the form of an ascension toward the infinite-One, which is the modern form of Aristotle's One-as-pure-act.

2. In this fourth orientation, being is given, not as the transcendence of the One-God, whether rational or ecstatic, but as the totality of itself, which incorporates multiple

expressions of itself, all immanent to its own unicity. This orientation receives its sendoff in Parmenides, who from the inexistence of non-being draws the conclusion of the absolute-oneness of being, of which all apparent existents are like unreal facets. The speculative culmination of this vision is obviously realized in Spinoza's system, in which is demonstrated the unicity of Substance (or Nature), which dispenses from within itself multiple modes whose whole being derives from the substantial One. Hegel proposes a dynamic version of the immanent orientation: being, qua absolute, is identical to its own multiform becoming. Being is the dialectical becoming of itself, and absolute Knowledge proceeds from a circular recapitulation of this becoming.

3. In the fifth orientation, being is given as thinkable only by forgoing all transcendence of the One as well as every unifying totalization. Being, in effect, is pure dispersion of the multiple, against the backdrop of the void. Put otherwise: the One (the void) is on the side of non-being, whereas being is the atomistic dissemination of itself. Since Democritus, this is the orientation that we can call "materialist," insofar as it forgoes every general meaning of being, in favor of the materiality of atoms and their combination in the void. Epicurus and Lucretius reclaim this tradition.

4. The sixth orientation, finally, affirms that the true thinking of being resides neither in the transcendent One nor in the immanent One, nor in the atomistic dispersion, since being has no other being than in relationality and the movements that transform and connect the relations among themselves. In other words, being is made of rela-

tions between relations. This is the position of Heraclitus, and closer to us, of Nietzsche, Bergson, or Deleuze. Today it finds sustenance in the mathematics of category theory. In particular, the theory of categories proposes a diagrammatic thinking of being as Relation of relations among relations. Such is the orientation that is summed up in the fundamental concept of functor, and its systemic orientation into sheaves.

It is with regard to the complexity of this philosophical legacy, concerning what an ontology can accomplish, that I had to choose my own orientation, armed with a vision of my own about the contemporary state of the conditions of philosophy. Of course, "choose" here is merely metaphorical: the orientation imposes itself upon a philosopher-subject, rather than being chosen in all tranquility among the six possibilities. And it imposed itself on me, due to my conviction that it was necessary to propose a "materialist" ontology, foreign to all transcendence, and yet capable of doing without the inconsistent concept of "matter," which only ever designates the hidden—and ultimately unthinkable—One of the evident multiplicity of all that is. This conviction came to me more from politics than from mathematics. And just as the young Marx already found himself obliged to do, it is then that I turned to the fifth orientation: the affirmation that being is nothing but pure multiplicity, without-One, and devoid of any specific attribute, whether of the type "matter" or "spirit."

What is crucial is that only from within this movement of thought did I come back to the mathematical condition, in order to see if it allowed me to find as rigorous as possible a structuring principle for my speculative decision. And I found this in set theory, because I interpreted this theory, specifically in its formalization of the ZFC type,[1] as being nothing less than the systematic study of all the possible forms of multiplicities, without-One, and without particularizing quality. I then returned to the field of philosophy, armed with a possible formal foundation of my primordial ontological decision.

We thus have a sort of circular path, which implicates the history of philosophy as to the ontological question, my being as a subject-in-philosophy, the current state of the mathematical condition, and once again my being-a-philosopher, who will incorporate himself into the history of philosophy about the ontological question. This circularity can also be expressed as follows: the state of ontological possibilities; the philosophical decision (taken by me) with regard to these possibilities; the retroactive movement back to the mathematical condition; the philosophico-mathematical decision to locate in this condition an adequate form for the ontological decision; investment of this second decision with the first, by way of the mathematical formalization of the concept of the multiple without-One and its variants; and the incorporation into the history of philosophy of a supposedly new ontological proposition (the book *Being and Event*).

In this circular movement, to be sure, it is impossible to examine separately my use of mathematics and my philosophical decision. But it is equally impossible to draw from it the equation "ontology = mathematics." Because the statement of the initial decision, namely, "being is multiplicity

---

[1] *Translator's note*: "ZFC" stands for the formalization of set theory named after Ernst Zermelo and Abraham Fraenkel, plus the axiom of choice.

without-One," by no means is a mathematical statement. And the detour via modern set theory does not serve as proof of the validity of this initial statement. The organized alliance between mathematics and philosophy is strong only if we observe its consequences. And it is only when we are already rather far into these consequences that one can truly appreciate the impact of such an alliance. In mathematics, one must be at least up to the level of Cohen's theorems regarding the generic subsets. And in philosophy, the speculative breadth of my project can be deciphered only in the dialectic between being and event, which means: between axiomatic determination and genericity, or again, between the multiplicities that are singularized by precise properties and the multiplicities universalized by their subtraction from all such properties.

IV. BEING AND EVENT

This long preamble allows me to come back, under renewed circumstances, to a central question, which even today is still highly disputed and criticized: what is, in the final instance, the exact function of set theory in the philosophical discourse that is my own?

One can answer this question as follows. The mathematical system of ZFC proposes to the philosopher a clear and rigorous scientific knowledge of all possible forms of pure multiplicity (without-One and devoid of empirical predicates such as "matter," "spirit," "atoms," "flux," etc.). These forms are defined exclusively by anonymous elements (or "sets"), to the exclusion of anything else, since the elements of a set are equally sets. There is no definition of what is a set, which is consistent with the function of sets that is to be pure forms of being, constituted by nothing other than other forms of being. The "donation" of the forms takes place only with the aid of axioms that specify certain relational properties, necessary for the identification of what such a form entails. The basic relation, called "belonging" and written ∈, serves, for example, in the written formula $x \in y$, to inscribe that the set x is an element of the set y. The relation ∈ can be considered as unique: every other relation in ZFC indeed must be defined on its basis, in the formal context of classical logic. Finally, the axiomatics fixes the properties of the relation ∈ in a determinate logical context and from there allows the definition of all kinds of other properties of the set-forms of pure multiplicity, of the kind "being transitive," "being infinite," "being well-founded," "being an ordinal," "being the set of the parts of another set," "being a function," "being generic," "being an inaccessible cardinal," etc. All these properties give the philosopher the means of conceptual movement, with great suppleness, in what are the resources of being qua being that thus becomes activated in the philosophical domain by the stimulus of mathematics.

One will ask why it is necessary for this speculative exploration of the ontological resources to keep on moving—as Aristotle already said in book Gamma of his *Metaphysics*—in the context of classical logic, which is a context essentially defined by the principle of non-contradiction (one cannot affirm at the same time the proposition p and the proposition not-p) and by the principle of the excluded middle (supposing a proposition p that is well formed, then either p is true or else it is true that not-p; there is no third position). The philosophical response to this question says the following: the majority of the propositions of ontology demand, as Parmenides has shown in a majestic fashion, the passage through the reasoning from the absurd. Parmenides in effect begins his speculative trajectory by affirming that it is impossible to demonstrate directly that only being is, but one can establish this proposition by showing that non-being is not. Following in the same school, in set theory one frequently observes that it is not possible to demonstrate directly the existence of such or such a form of the pure multiple. For a number of forms there can be no proof of their existence that would be constructive and if possible intuitive. On the other hand, we can obtain results of the following kind: "If I deny the existence of this form of the multiple, it follows that I must also deny the validity of a proposition that I previously demonstrated to be true." The reasoning from the absurd thus allows us to conclude that said form of the multiple exists. One can—one must—also admit a rule of maximum tolerance, which can be formulated thus: "If this form of the multiple, for example a certain type of infinite multiplicity, can be clearly defined in the formal language, as long as I have no proof of the negation of its existence, I can—in fact, I must—admit its existence." The whole point is that the fundamental relation of belonging, or $\in$, is marked ontologically by the seal of classical logic. Indeed, given a set x and a set y, either $x \in y$ or else not-$(x \in y)$. There is no third hypothesis, and we thus operate under the law of the excluded third, characteristic of classical logic. My speculative statement will therefore be: ontology is classical.

Now, I must also show that the axioms of classical set theory, the theory of ZFC, may claim a philosophical legitimacy. I have done so, I believe conscientiously, for the totality of the axioms of the ZFC system. I will pick only three examples, which bear on the most contested axioms, including among certain philosophers.

Ontology and Mathematics 61

For example, for reasons that are properly ontological, I validate the formidable, counterintuitive, and often deplored "axiom of choice," which is one of the important characteristics of the ZFC system. This axiom says that, given a set of sets—which is the case, let us recall, of any set—there exists always a function that allows me to exhibit one and only one element of each of these sets, and this is so without exception. In other words, given a set A, with the elements $x_1, x_2, x_3 \ldots x_n, x_{n+1} \ldots$, there exists a function F, called the function of choice, which "extracts" from each of the elements $x_1, x_2, x_3 \ldots x_n, x_{n+1} \ldots$, one and only one element of this element. In sum, we have $F(A)$ such that for every x_n of A, we have one $y_n \in F(A)$ such that y_n is the sole element of $F(A)$ that is an element of x_n. The function F "chooses" *one* element of each of the elements of A. Thus, $F(A)$ is like a national assembly of the representatives of the elements of A, one elected official per element, with F being in a way the electoral procedure for designating these representatives.

The axiom of choice poses no electoral problem as long as one manages finite sets. But in the infinite, how can we define a function that associates one representative to each element of the infinity of elements of the initial set? Most often, one cannot prove the existence of a well-defined procedure capable of extracting an infinite set from such an infinity of representatives. The axiom of choice has been contested because it affirms the existence of a procedure that one cannot manage to produce. In reality, in the case of infinite sets, the axiom of choice affirms the existence of a particular infinity, which is the result of the simultaneous choice of an element of each of the elements, in infinite number, of the initial set. But the existence of this set cannot, in general, be proven or constructed, and its existence is then guaranteed, by way of the axiom of choice, only as an *a priori* principle.

I nonetheless admit this axiom for three philosophical reasons.

The first is what I call the principle of maximality: the materialist ontology posits that every well-defined form of the multiple must be accepted as possibly real in a world, until there is proof of the contrary. Any restriction of the existence of forms of the multiple is ontologically unacceptable, if its reasons concern only the capacity of our finite minds effectively to construct their elements. This would mean relapsing in a form of relativistic empiricism. Our impotence to construct a form of multiple being should not be a reason for refusing its existence. Lacking a counter-example, the axiom of choice must be taken to be valid. It presents us with a multiplicity clearly defined as "representative" of another multiplicity, which in itself is interesting and has turned out to be necessary in the actual practice of modern analysis.

The second reason is logical. By way of the beautiful axiom of Diaconescu, which operates in the context of category theory, the axiom of choice imposes that the logical context be classical, as we desire. The negation of the axiom of choice would thus open the possibility that our logic might not be classical, which is ontologically unacceptable.

The third reason is closer to meta-mathematics: Gödel has proven that if the ZF theory (without the axiom of choice) is consistent (without internal contradiction), then the ZFC theory (with the axiom of choice) is as well. The admission of the axiom of choice does not introduce by itself any particular risk.

As an example of the principle of maximality, guarantee of logical classicism, and conformity to the consistency of the context, the axiom of choice is a precious principle of speculative ontology.

Here is a second example. I accept, for a major philosophical reason, the axiom of foundation. This axiom says that every set possesses at least one element (or several) that has (or have) no element in common with the initial set. For those who find formulae clearer than sentences, we can write the axiom of foundation as follows:

> For every set x: $\forall x$
> There exists at least one set y: $\exists y$
> Such that it is an element of the initial set: $y \in x$
> And such that if z is an element of y: $z \in y$
> Then z is not an element of the initial set: $z \notin x$.

After which, you can punctuate all that in a legible manner in a single formula, which you will note is infinitely shorter than the same statement in the mother tongue:

$$(\forall x)(\exists y)[(y \in x) \text{ and } (z \in y) \to (z \notin x)]$$

The exceptional importance of this axiom in the philosophical field—and already in the conditions of political or amorous truth—stems from the fact that it affirms the following: ontologically, the Other is present within every Identity. Every multiple form, indeed, admits within itself an element whose own composition and multiple-being are foreign to it. We can also say that the axiom of foundation affirms the immanence of negativity: there is a point of being in every multiple form that is not of the domain of this form itself. It follows, in my philosophy of truths, that *nothing true can be strictly identitarian*. Ontologically, the *pure* totality is therefore always false, which from a political point of view has extraordinary consequences. The element z marks the position of radical alterity: against all racism and identitarianism, for example, the Other is always lodged within identity. Given that mathematics is not a normative discipline, ontology here has no normativity either. It simply says: with regard to being, which is neutral, nonnormative, and thought in its absolute generality, alterity is always present in it. To say that all the French are purely French is thus ontologically false. We are dealing with an originary and irreducible admixture, so why fall back on an identity? The horizon is universality. In other words, "truth" and "universality" are inseparable.

From the axiom of foundation, it follows that one can never obtain the purely reflexive statement $x \in x$. This can be demonstrated without major difficulty. It means, philosophically, that no multiple form can be an element of the multiple form that it is—which, in sum, is fairly evident: ontologically, the form is a battle against the formless qua non-being, and, in this battle, it cannot affirm itself as already being itself by and in itself. We can also interpret the absolute impossibility of the statement $(x \in x)$ from the side of the theory of the subject. This impossibility then can be expressed as follows: there exists no reflexivity that would be integral. Or again: every cogito is partial. Here you may think of Freud and of the unconscious: you never totally belong to yourself.

Third example. I finally accept without any restriction the axiom of the infinite, which affirms the existence of an infinite set (and, under the effect of the other axioms, the existence of an infinite series of types of infinities).

Ontology and Mathematics 65

This axiom amounts to saying that there exist forms of the multiple that are infinite, but it can do so only by defining with precision a concept of the infinite. There exist several ways of proposing such a definition. They are all operative in their essence and avoid the vague and para-intuitive approaches of the kind "the infinite is what is very big." The most common among these definitions consists in defining an operation that works on the sets and indicating that this operation can be reiterated, without any halting point.

Thus, let there be a set x, absolutely any whatsoever, and the set whose only element is x, which one calls the singleton of x, written $\{x\}$. In passing you will note that x is necessarily different from the singleton $\{x\}$, for the following reason: if one has $x = \{x\}$, it follows that the set $\{x\}$ does not obey the axiom of foundation. Indeed, following this axiom, there should be an element of the singleton that has no element in common with the singleton itself. But the sole element of the singleton is x. Thus, there must be an element of x that is not an element of the singleton. If the singleton is equal to x, we end up in the absurdity according to which there exists an element of x that is not an element of x. We thus always have, since we assume the axiom of choice: $\{x\} \neq x$.

In these conditions let us affirm the existence of a set Inf, such that if we have $x \in$ Inf, then we also always have $\{x\} \in$ Inf. It is clear that in so doing, we open a reiteration without any halting point, of the type: x, $\{x\}$, $\{\{x\}\}$, ..., ..., which is "wholly" contained within Inf. We thus will agree that Inf is an infinite form of the multiple.

One absolutely fundamental property of infinite sets is that a strict part of these sets may be as big as the set itself. The axiom of Greek mathematics, "the whole is larger than the parts," is not valid for the infinite forms of the multiple. It is actually easy to see, based on the most intuitive example of an infinite set, namely, the set of positive whole numbers, our good old "natural" numbers—1, 2, 3, and so on—that the supposed axiom "the whole is larger than the parts" is false in the infinite, as Galileo had already observed with great forcefulness. Indeed, there exist for example as many even numbers as there are numbers, period. You simply establish a correspondence between any number and double this number. To 1 corresponds 2, to 2 corresponds 4, and so on, so that to the grand total of whole numbers 1, 2, 3 . . . n, $n+1$ . . . there corresponds exactly the total of even numbers 2, 4, 6 . . . $2n$, $2(n+1)$. And this is the case, although the even numbers are a strict part of the whole numbers. Well, this part is as large as the whole.

Furthermore, one major reason for admitting the axiom of the infinite is in my view to engage oneself in a study of the forms of the multiple that exceeds our intuitions, generally limited to the finite. Here too, in sum, the principle of maximality must prevail: of everything that is clearly defined, without formal contradiction, we must affirm the existence, since our elementary intuitions have no reason to be the measure of being qua being.

However, ontology defined under the condition of this part of mathematics that studies the different forms of the pure multiple does not create by itself the possibility of knowing that which is the creation of a particular truth in a particular world. Certainly, there is a need for the thinking of the forms of the multiple, of what the being of all that is may be. In fact, every science is mathematical, more or less. Even Lacan concludes that psychoanalysis has the matheme as its ideal. And yet, every theory of truths, and of the subject of truths, armed with a thinking of being as such, must also inscribe its proposal within the singularity of a world and of what it proposes in terms of materials for a creative type of thinking.

Philosophy thus must draw from its conditions, and turn into concepts, a general theory of what in a singular world may be a process that is subjectivized with a universal value. But first of all, what is a world? Naturally, a world is ontologically composed of a multiplicity, endowed with a definable form, itself composed of multiplicities of which mathematics may be able to conceptualize the forms. But what is the exact nature, or the singularity, of this "composition"?

V. LOGICS OF WORLDS

The aim of *Logics of Worlds* is to propose an answer to this question, and since then I consider it impossible to separate *Being and Event* from *Logics of Worlds*, just as more recently it has become impossible to separate the former from *The Immanence of Truths*. Indeed, we cannot separate the universality of truths, established in *Being and Event*, from their singularity, the thought of which is worked out in *Logics of Worlds*, and from their absoluteness, reflected in *The Immanence of Truths*.

Here I can only present a few general features of *Logics of Worlds*, with the aim of clarifying some of the uses of mathematics in the book.

- The central concept of the whole book is that of *identity within a given world (or also, dialectically, difference within a given world)*. The ontological concept of identity is strictly extensional: two forms of the multiple are different if, and only if, there exists at least one element that belongs to one of the forms and not to the other. If this is not the case, they are identical. The "worldly" concept of identity, and thus of difference, is by contrast intentional, qualitative, and relative to the world under consideration. A set x and a set y belonging to the same world are affected, as a pair, by a variable *degree of identity*, between a minimum μ (the two objects are, in this world, totally different) and a maximum M (the two objects are, in this world, practically identical). The different possible values of the degrees of identity are drawn from an object of the world affected by a structure of order, which is *the transcendental* of the world in question.

- A set belonging to a world, seen from the angle of its degrees of identity with all the other elements of the same world, is an *object* of this world. One thus can see that a set that is an element of the totality of the world—a world that itself is also, in its being, a set—is not a sufficient definition of what is an object, for the simple reason that belonging to a set is a purely ontological determination. To define objectivity, we must take into consideration the qualitative and variable concept of the differential degree of identity, which in general is extremely variable.

- An object of the world *is*, of course, but it also *exists*. The presence of an object in a determinate world is itself affected by a degree, which is *the degree of identity of the object under consideration with itself*. This degree defines the *existence* of the object in a world. If the existence is maximal (the degree of existence of the object is M), the object exists in the world "absolutely." If by contrast the existence is minimal (the degree is μ), the object is not absent from the world, since its being as a set belongs to the being of the world, but *it is an inexistent of the world*. The intermediate degrees attach themselves to existences in the world that are more or less intense.

To explain all this in an extremely simplified way, I need a few preliminary comments. Let us call "an entity," or "a being," as in Heidegger, any multiplicity whatsoever, and let us focus on the appearing of this entity, on what allows us to say that this entity exists in a determinate world. Let us suppose that we tried to think of the entity not only according to its being—that is, according to the pure multiplicity that constitutes its being, without determination—but insofar as it is there—that is, insofar as it occurs or appears against the horizon of a world. Let us call this appearing within a world the "existence" of this entity. To the extent that an entity is an undifferentiated multiplicity, we will be interested in the worldly horizon that makes this entity into something that, aside from being the multiplicity that it is, which is mathematically thinkable, appears against the horizon of a world. There where it appears in a world, it exists. Consequently, we install ourselves in a wholly classical distinction between being and existence, albeit slightly transformed. Indeed, "being" in this case is that which can be thought of as pure multiplicity, and "existence," that which can be thought of as being-there of this multiplicity, against the horizon of a constituted world or a determinate world.

The technical elaboration of this can take very different paths. There can be no question of our entering into the details, but allow me to say simply that the passage from being to existence, the relation between being and being-there, or the relation between multiplicity and the worldly inscription of multiplicity constitutes a transcendental relation. The latter consists precisely of the fact that within a world any multiplicity is assigned a degree of existence, or a degree of appearance. We must understand that the fact of existing, as an appearance in a determinate world, inevitably is associated with a certain degree, a certain intensity of appearing in this world, which we can also call the intensity of existence. Thus, multiplicity transcendentally will be given—that is the transcendental relation—an intensity of existence, which assigns it to a determinate world. Of course—this is a complicated but important point—a multiplicity may appear in several different worlds. We admit a principle of ubiquity of being, I would even go so far as to say that this is what defines humanity. Why can humanity present itself as superior to all the rest? Exclusively because of its capacity to appear in a great many different worlds, of being assigned transcendentally to extraordinarily different degrees of existence. We exist in several worlds, fortunately! Because if we were bolted to one world, it would be extraordinarily painful, especially if the world in question were evil, which is generally the case.

A multiplicity thus can appear in several worlds, and as a general rule it appears with different degrees of intensity: intensely in one world, weakly in another, extremely weakly in a third, with an extraordinary intensity in a fourth. Existentially we are very familiar with this circulation between the different worlds in which we inscribe ourselves with different intensities. Each one of us knows that such sequences of existence often mark the passage of a world in which we exist with a weak degree of existence to a world in which we exist with a more intense degree of existence: that is what is called a vital moment. For all this there exists a sophisticated logic.

Ontology and Mathematics

The crucial point is the following: supposing a multiplicity that appears in a world, and supposing the elements of this multiplicity that appear, if I may say so, at the same time with it, then insofar as the totality of what constitutes it appears in the world, there always exists a component of this multiplicity whose appearance is measured by the weakest degree, that is to say, it exists minimally. You will understand that existing minimally in the transcendental of a world is like not existing at all. A divine eye, external to the world, could eventually compare the minimums. But if you are in the world, then to exist the least possible way means, from the point of view of the world, not to exist at all. This is why we will call this element "the inexistent." At that point, it is easy to state the following: supposing a multiplicity that appears in a world, there is always an element of this multiplicity that is inexistent in this world. It is the inexistent proper to this multiplicity, relative to this world. But we must be careful: the inexistent has no ontological definition; it only has an existential definition, namely, that it is a minimal degree of existence. What is interesting is that this can be demonstrated. I will not give you the demonstration, but you can search for it yourselves. It is possible to demonstrate that there is always, in that which appears, a point that is the inexistent. If the multiplicity is called A, the point of inexistence will be marked thus: $\emptyset A$, that is, the empty set, index A. This is a proper name, meaning the inexistent of A. And you will remember that the inexistent of A is always the inexistent that is proper to A in a given world.

I will give you a broad and well-known example. In Marx's analysis of bourgeois and capitalist societies, the proletariat is the inexistent proper to the political multiplicities. It is what does not exist, which does not mean that it has no being. There always has been this confusion. Marx obviously does not mean to say that the proletariat has no being, since on the contrary he fills volume upon volume to explain what it is. The social being of the proletariat is not in question. For Marx, the proletariat is completely subtracted from the whole business of political representation, in the extent to which its being, the multiplicity that it is, is in the world, absolutely, and can be analyzed. But if we take the rules of appearing in the political world, we find that the proletariat does not appear in it. It is in this world, but with a minimal degree of appearance, namely, zero degree of appearance. This is what is sung in "The International": "We are nothing, let us be all!" Those who say "we are nothing" obviously are not affirming their nothingness; they are affirming that they are nothing in the world as it is, when it is a question of appearing politically. From the point of view of their political appearing, they are nothing. And the becoming-all presupposes the changing of the world, the changing of the transcendental: there must be a change in the transcendental for the assignation to a certain degree of existence itself to be modified. Thus, the inexistence is precisely the point of non-appearing of a multiplicity in a world, a point relative to the transcendental of this world. You yourselves will be able to find many other examples. I insist on this: it is a general law of appearing, of being-there, that it always summons forth a point of inexistence.

- The global logic of this whole theoretical arsenal concerning objects obviously presupposes set theory (the being of an object of the world is established by its belonging, qua set, to a form of the multiple that is the world), but its core resides rather in the formal theory of relations that is the *theory of categories*. An object indeed is existentially defined as such by its variable relations with all the objects of the world, including itself (by the determination of its degree of existence in the world). Given that we have passed from being (thinkable in an absolute generality) to existence (being as contextualized in a particular world), that is, from ontology (being qua being, *pure* multiplicities) to logic (the relations that are woven between all the things that appear locally in worlds), we can calculate a degree of existence: a differential determination of these relations on a scale of intensities.

- Some more technical considerations, drawn from the fundamental notions of category theory, allow us to conclude that *a world possesses globally the structure of a Grothendieck topos*. Incidentally, I note in passing that we can speak of a *topos*, for example, if a form of being is a form of the world. An event happens always to a world: every event is *localized*, and thus all truth is localized, even if it can happen in other worlds (whence its universality), and even if it is in a world based on something that does not belong to the world (whence its genericity).

There are thus as many reasons to say that for me "relation" or "action" or "existence in a world," or again "identity and difference," which are major concepts in all forms of vitalism, belong to category theory as there are to say that my ontology is set theory. But, in both cases, a philosophical concept, without a fixed mathematical concept, remains at the heart of the circular relation between philosophy and its mathematical condition. This concept, in the latter case, is "being as multiplicity without-One" and, in the former, "appearing in the world as intensity of existence."

In *Being and Event*, the philosophical concept of universality is ontologically supported by the mathematical concept of *generic* set. *A generic set is a subset of a given infinite set, which cannot be defined by a common property of its elements, a property available in the repertoire of definable properties in the world within which one operates.* In other words, on the one hand, you have an infinite set, let us say A, and, on the other hand, the properties P definable within ZFC with the aid of the existing constants, logical operators, and the relation $\in$. A subset of A will be "generic" if it is not defined, using the axiom of separation, by any of the available properties P whatsoever. So, it will be "generic" if it is a subset G of A, but is not defined, nor definable, as "the set of elements of A that have the property P." Finally, we can say that the sole property of G is that of being a subset of A. It is in this sense that it is a generic subset, a "pure" subset, not linked to this or that property available in the language of theory.

I have shown that here we have potentially a formalization of the distinction that is particularly important for Hegel between "knowledge" and "truth": knowledge is a property common to various things of the world, a property expressed in the dominant language. A truth is a creation "outside knowledge," inexpressible as such at the moment of its creation, in the dominant language (and thus often refused by the tenacious partisans of this language). On this point we cross paths with the Platonic opposition between "opinion" and "true knowledge." The first is always already circulating in all shared statements; the second demands a radical movement of purification, at the center of which we begin to see the profile of an Idea.

It becomes easy to understand that in the ontology of the multiple, the basis for opinions or common knowledge would be a subset of the situation subtracted from this situation by the axiom of separation, thus by the union of all the multiples that have the same property, which itself is mapped out for all in the dominant language. But also, that if there is such as a thing as the creation of a truth, it requires the support at the level of being of a generic subset, indifferent to the dominant language.

In the early 1960s Paul Cohen discovered a general method for producing generic sets, which consists in a set-theoretical model based on the ZFC theory. For me, this constitutes the foundation at last discovered, at the level of pure being, of what is a *universal* truth, since a generic set goes beyond all the mappable identities of the existing world.

As for the concept of *singularity*, its status is clearly defined in the context of the theory of *topoi*, which is a subsection of the theory of categories, by way of the concept of an object's existence in a world. Finally, the ancient distinction between "universality" and "singularity" is elucidated, under the condition of different mathematical frameworks (the ZFC theory, the theory of *topoi*), first by way of the distinction between multiple-being and existence-in-a-world, and then by the more technical distinction between "generic set" on the one hand, and "relational degree of existence" in a world, on the other.

In my first two books of contemporary metaphysics, I thus made it possible to distinguish the universality of truths (genericity) and their singularity (existence) in relation to a given world of opinions. But what remains to be understood is how one can sustain that truths are absolute, that is to say, not only opposed to all empiricist interpretation but also guaranteed against any transcendental construction, which means endowed with a being that is independent from the subject or subjects that nevertheless were their historical agents in specific worlds.

Let us phrase this otherwise. In *Being and Event*, I show how the universal exception of a truth can surge forth, by way of an event, in the guise of a generic multiplicity. In *Logics of Worlds*, I show that truths, whose *being* is exceptional, also have an *existence*, as singularities, as finite works, in really-existing worlds. Thus, I can guarantee the ontological possibility of multiplicities that are sufficiently distant from the world in which they happen to have a universal value. And I can guarantee, on the other hand, that the universality of a work of truth does not exclude that it is the result of particular operations, the original materials for which have existed in a particular world.

Finally:

- With the ontological framework of *pure multiplicity*, I escape the dominance of transcendence, or of the One, as the sole guarantee of the being of truth.

- With the framework of *generic universality*, I have left behind both empiricism and relativism, which deny the existence of universal truths.

- With the theory of the *existence in a world* of the construction of generic truths, and thus of their *singularity*, I have left behind idealism, which attempts to extract the power of the true from any world whatsoever to make it into a completely subjective process.

Now, against the dominance of perspectivism, we still must establish another point, which is the following: the fact that truths depend, in terms of their emergence, on the scaffolding of an event and that their being is generic does not at all prohibit that, once they are put to work in a given world, they may be absolute in a precise sense. And, in relation to the mathematical condition of philosophy, this sense does not follow either from Cohen's procedures of forcing or from the subtleties of the theory of *topoi*, but from yet another sector of fundamental mathematics, which is the theory of infinities, still in full expansion over the last decades. This is what defines the stakes of my third book, *The Immanence of Truths*.

VI. THE IMMANENCE OF TRUTHS

I can only sketch out the approach of this last book in terms of the relation between philosophy and its mathematical condition.

The ontological universality does not guarantee in and of itself the absoluteness of truths. The relativist can always claim that it is merely the guarantee of a possible circulation of a work in its generic support from one world to another, or even the imperialist imposition of a local genericity onto heterogeneous cultural worlds. My friend Barbara Cassin, for instance, raised this objection to me. "Universality is always the universality of someone," she told me, with the somewhat naïve force that always results from a fusion between empiricism (the supposed universality as a sensible and cultural thing, a fact of language) and idealism (everything exists "for someone").

In substance, my third book responds to this objection by arguing that the absoluteness of truth is itself guaranteed by the type of infinity with which the setting to work of the truth—which is always, ontologically, a finite fragment of a generic and therefore universal becoming—enters into a relation. The heart of *The Immanence of Truths* consists in elucidating the nature of this immanent relation between the work of truth and the infinite, which constitutes the foundation for the absoluteness of the true.

Of course, I fully expect that Barbara Cassin, using the example of religions, will reply that "absoluteness is always the absoluteness of someone." But a work of truth is something that exists in different worlds and thus has nothing to do with a religion. A revolution, a love, a painting, a theorem: they are there, for everyone to see. And everyone in the end can see in them the invariance of what has a universal value, because all participate, in the subjective experience that confronts them in such works, in the relation between the finite work and the latent infinity of its being.

Of the mathematical meditation of this point, which is particularly complex, I can give at most a general idea that I hope to be clear. Let us say that the contemporary theory of infinities authorizes us to define philosophically what is an *attribute of the absolute*. The absolute, for its part, can only be formal in the eyes of the mathematician: it is the collection, which is mentally situatable (definable) but logically inconsistent, of all possible forms of the multiple without-One.

Let us note in passing that mathematics, with the intuitive brilliance that always characterizes it, has given the name of V to this absolute, which though logically inconsistent, nevertheless exists sufficiently for us to be able to describe some of its properties. This name no doubt can be taken to mean many things: Great Void, but also Place of Truths (or Verities).

What "infinitizes" and thus absolutizes a work of truth that in its real existence is at once finite, singular (existing), and universal (generic) is its mediated link with the absolute. This mediation is assured by one of the attributes in which really-existing works in particular worlds may "participate"—as is the case of Spinoza's decisive intuitions in this regard, when he defines the "attributes of Substance." The stroke of genius of mathematics on this topic has been to give a clear definition of what constitutes such an attribute of the absolute. Its mathematical name is *transitive class of V (the absolute), onto which there exists an elementary embedding of the absolute itself.*

Here I cannot go into the exact meaning of this definition, even if, as is always the case in mathematics, the underlying idea is clearer than the calculations that support its validity. Nonetheless, the definition exists. What is more, we know of a fundamental condition for the existence of at least one attribute of the absolute: it is the existence of a "very large" infinity (a "large cardinal," as the anglophones say) of a special type, which I call "complete" for a series of solid philosophical reasons.

Still by way of a tightly knit circulation between philosophy and mathematics, I thus have been able to show that the (mathematical) definition of what in philosophy I rename an "attribute of the absolute" clearly supports the speculative sense I give to this notion. All that is left to do for the philosophers, whoever they are, is to enter the difficult detours of the construction of infinities and to find in it the path toward an absolutization of the works of truth, about which I have already shown, in my back and forth between philosophy and mathematics, that they are at the same time singular and universal, and about which all that remains to be proven is that they are also absolute.

I believe I managed to do so. I did this at a sufficiently advanced age for this accomplishment to be truly comforting! Allow me to end with this proud assertion!

Cultural Memory | *in the Present*

Eric Song, *Love Against Substitution: Seventeenth-Century English Literature and the Meaning of Marriage*

Niklaus Largier, *Figures of Possibility: Aesthetic Experience, Mysticism, and the Play of the Senses*

Mihaela Mihai, *Political Memory and the Aesthetics of Care: The Art of Complicity and Resistance*

Ethan Kleinberg, *Emmanuel Levinas's Talmudic Turn: Philosophy and Jewish Thought*

Willemien Otten, *Thinking Nature and the Nature of Thinking: From Eriugena to Emerson*

Michael Rothberg, *The Implicated Subject: Beyond Victims and Perpetrators*

Hans Ruin, *Being with the Dead: Burial, Ancestral Politics, and the Roots of Historical Consciousness*

Eric Oberle, *Theodor Adorno and the Century of Negative Identity*

David Marriott, *Whither Fanon? Studies in the Blackness of Being*

Reinhart Koselleck, *Sediments of Time: On Possible Histories*, translated and edited by Sean Franzel and Stefan-Ludwig Hoffmann

Devin Singh, *Divine Currency: The Theological Power of Money in the West*

Stefanos Geroulanos, *Transparency in Postwar France: A Critical History of the Present*

Sari Nusseibeh, *The Story of Reason in Islam*

Olivia C. Harrison, *Transcolonial Maghreb: Imagining Palestine in the Era of Decolonialization*

Barbara Vinken, *Flaubert Postsecular: Modernity Crossed Out*

Aishwary Kumar, *Radical Equality: Ambedkar, Gandhi, and the Problem of Democracy*

Simona Forti, *New Demons: Rethinking Power and Evil Today*

Joseph Vogl, *The Specter of Capital*

Hans Joas, *Faith as an Option*

Michael Gubser, *The Far Reaches: Ethics, Phenomenology, and the Call for Social Renewal in Twentieth-Century Central Europe*

Françoise Davoine, *Mother Folly: A Tale*

Knox Peden, *Spinoza Contra Phenomenology: French Rationalism from Cavaillès to Deleuze*

Elizabeth A. Pritchard, *Locke's Political Theology: Public Religion and Sacred Rights*

Ankhi Mukherjee, *What Is a Classic? Postcolonial Rewriting and Invention of the Canon*

Jean-Pierre Dupuy, *The Mark of the Sacred*

Henri Atlan, *Fraud: The World of Ona'ah*

Niklas Luhmann, *Theory of Society, Volume 2*

Ilit Ferber, *Philosophy and Melancholy: Benjamin's Early Reflections on Theater and Language*

Alexandre Lefebvre, *Human Rights as a Way of Life: On Bergson's Political Philosophy*

Theodore W. Jennings, Jr., *Outlaw Justice: The Messianic Politics of Paul*

Alexander Etkind, *Warped Mourning: Stories of the Undead in the Land of the Unburied*

Denis Guénoun, *About Europe: Philosophical Hypotheses*

Maria Boletsi, *Barbarism and Its Discontents*

Sigrid Weigel, *Walter Benjamin: Images, the Creaturely, and the Holy*

Roberto Esposito, *Living Thought: The Origins and Actuality of Italian Philosophy*

Henri Atlan, *The Sparks of Randomness, Volume 2: The Atheism of Scripture*

Rüdiger Campe, *The Game of Probability: Literature and Calculation from Pascal to Kleist*